CIVIL WAR CHRONICLES

FROM AUCTION BLOCK
TO GLORY

CIVIL WAR CHRONICLES

FROM AUCTION BLOCK TO GLORY

The African American Experience

PHILLIP THOMAS TUCKER, PH.D.

MetroBooks

MetroBooks

An Imprint of Friedman/Fairfax Publishers

© 1998 by Michael Friedman Publishing Group, Inc.

Library of Congress Cataloging-in-Publication Data

Tucker, Phillip Thomas
        From auction block to glory: the African American experience in
the Civil War / by Phillip Thomas Tucker.
                p.   cm. — (The Civil War chronicles)
        Includes bibliographical references and index.
        ISBN 1-56799-552-7
        1. United States — History — Civil War, 1861-1865 — Afro-Americans.
2. Afro-Americans — History — To 1863. 3. Afro-Americans-
- History — 1863-1877. [1. United States — History — Civil War,
1861-1865 — Participation, Afro-American.] I. Title. II. Series:
Civil War chronicles (MetroBooks (Firm))
E540.N3T83   1998
973.7'1 — dc21   97-18180

Editors: Tony Burgess and Ann Kirby
Art Director: Kevin Ullrich
Photography Editor: Amy Talluto
Production Manager: Camille Lee

Color separations by Bright Arts Graphics Pte Ltd
Printed in China by Leefung—Asco Printers Ltd.

10 9 8 7 6 5 4 3 2 1

For bulk purchases and special sales, please contact:
Friedman / Fairfax Publishers
Attention: Sales Department
15 West 26th Street
New York, NY 10010
(212) 685-6610 FAX (212) 685-1307

Visit our website:
http://www.metrobooks.com

DEDICATION

For a special lady who contributed so much in so many ways,
Betty Jane Cox-Tucker.

ACKNOWLEDGMENTS

Many people have been responsible for my early interest in the
Civil War, especially my elder relatives, who passed down stories
about the hardships endured by my family during the conflict.
Originally from the hill country of North Carolina, the Tucker family
was living in Hardin County, Tennessee, during the war. In the early
spring of 1862, soldiers from both armies raided the Tucker farmstead
so thoroughly that the family would never forget it. Not far from the
family cabin, the bloody battle of Shiloh raged for two terrible days,
turning the bright spring forests, meadows, and fields of Hardin
County around the Shiloh Methodist Church a terrible shade of red.
I would like to thank those relatives, now long deceased, who
kindly took the time to tell their stories to a curious young boy
who was fascinated by what they had to say about events that
happened so long ago.

CONTENTS

INTRODUCTION
The Coming of War

He who serves his country well has
no need of ancestors.

—Voltaire

The American Civil War developed from fears on each side that the other might be able to dominate the American political process. The major difference between the two sections of the United States—populated by essentially the same people—involved the institution of slavery. In the northern portion of the nation, where slavery was less of an economic necessity, states had begun to free slave populations or refuse to allow any newborn African Americans to be made slaves as early as 1827. Either by emancipation or through policies that gradually eliminated the entire practice, slavery began to vanish from the North.

While the South had also considered the elimination of slavery as early as 1831, several factors prevented any such action from being taken. A large population of slaves—over 2.16 million—were living in the South, and serious social and economic concerns would undoubtedly arise should they be freed. First and foremost, the invention of the cotton gin had resulted in an increased demand for cotton as an export from the region, and as slaves were an integral part of the agricultural system that produced this

John Brown was the militant abolitionist who first won gory fame with a massacre of pro-South settlers at Pottowatomie Creek, Kansas. He helped to lead the way to war by polarizing the nation in the sectional struggle for Kansas during the 1850s, and then by his audacious capture of the United States Arsenal at Harpers Ferry, Virginia, in October 1859. After his capture, Brown was executed by hanging. He then became a martyr to the North and an infamous promoter of slave insurrection to the South. "John Brown's Body" was sung by Union soldiers, both black and white, when they marched through the South to victory.

commodity, there was a surge in the demand for slave labor in the fields. To free the slaves, then, would upset the economic structure, as slave labor would need to be replaced with paid labor. Second, these newly freed slaves would have to be integrated into society, needing food, shelter, and paid work. Further, slave rebellions were not uncommon in the South, and in nearby Haiti, a violent slave rebellion in the early 1800s had resulted in the murder or flight of most of the white population, and in the establishment of the first black republic in the New World. Many of the Haitian whites who fled settled in the southern United States, bringing with them tales of atrocities at the hands of rebel slaves. Fear of such a revolt, along with economic concerns and the daunting task of resettling large numbers of freed slaves into Southern society, were major factors behind the South's support of slavery as an accepted institution and a means of controlling the black population at a time when the North was choosing to free its relatively small black population.

The differences in regional policies were fueled by abolitionists in the North and secessionist "fire-eaters" in the South, both of whom kept the political pot boiling through crisis after crisis within the young nation. It was, however, the activities of one man that were soon to cause Americans to focus on their differences, rather than their similarities.

The horror of slavery: slave pens at a leading slave trading establishment in Alexandria, Virginia. The major Potomac River port city of Alexandria, immediately below Washington, D.C., was within sight of the nation's capital.

A fierce and militant abolitionist, John Brown, had gained a gory reputation from acts he and his followers committed in Kansas, and he was in the process of moving east.

Brown's 1859 capture of the Federal armory in Harpers Ferry was intended to seize arms to equip slaves who would rally to his revolutionary movement as he—like a modern Spartacus—led them to freedom. The failure of Brown's plan, and his subsequent trial, became nationally recognized flash points that further polarized relations between the two regions, as men in the South began to prepare for additional abolitionist-inspired attacks. Brown took immediate advantage of the publicity in national newspapers, stating, "I am worth inconceivably more to hang than for any other purpose."

With his execution by hanging, this man who used terrorism to push forward his political agenda was viewed as a near-saint by many Northerners. Ironically, "John Brown's Body" was soon a favorite marching song of the Union armies, which moved south, while the African Americans whom Brown had hoped to unite in freedom were painfully absent from the Union's marching columns.

Northern blacks had volunteered to serve in the Union army since the earliest days of the Civil War, but they had been refused by the War Department—even though blacks had served in all of the nation's earlier conflicts, including the American Revolution and the War of 1812—and the regular army didn't enlist black men. Attempts to organize black troops into regiments in Kansas and on the occupied coast of South Carolina were also rejected by the Republican administration.

One branch of the service, however, had accepted black volunteers from the beginning of the war. The Union navy had accepted all races from its first days, but blacks were normally used only in noncombat roles such as cooks, stewards, and firemen who stoked the boilers in the ships. Some groups of African American men were allowed to join or form gun crews in the early days of the war, but this was a rare occurrence. Only with the signing of the Emancipation Proclamation would significant numbers of African Americans begin to form combat units and participate actively in the Civil War.

Radical Republicans, abolitionists, and black leaders had been actively encouraging the use of black regiments throughout the war. The leading black spokesman, Frederick Douglass, wrote:

> Once let the black man get upon his person the brass letters "U.S."; let him get an eagle on his button, and a musket on his shoulder and bullets in his pocket, and there is no power on earth which can deny that he has earned the right to citizenship.

Others, however, had some reservations about the use of these new soldiers. President Abraham Lincoln himself initially expressed some uneasiness, telling visitors that "to arm the negroes would turn 50,000 bayonets against us that were for us."

But it was only a matter of time before significant numbers of black soldiers were

The infamous Fort Pillow Massacre. Fort Pillow, above Memphis, Tennessee, protected Federal shipping on "the Father of Waters." On bloody April 12, 1864, Confederate forces under General Nathan B. Forrest—a former Memphis slave trader and one of the war's great cavalry commanders—overran the fort after the defiant Federals refused to surrender. Shortly thereafter, General Forrest's Rebels captured the fort, killing blacks who had surrendered, including soldiers of the 11th United States Colored Infantry.

enrolled into the ranks of the Union army. Regiments were soon formed in Louisiana and Kansas, but it was in the North that the most highly visible regiments were raised. Massachusetts' abolitionist governor pressed the Federal government for permission to raise black regiments and was soon given the authority to do so. The Bureau of Colored Troops was formed in May 1863. Volunteers were organized into two regiments, the 54th and 55th Massachusetts, and these men—along with their white officers—were soon sent off to war.

Initially, black soldiers were enlisted to serve as laborers, prison guards, and similar noncombat military occupations that would allow additional white soldiers to be transferred into combat units. There was a genuine concern that, if captured while in combat against their former masters, black soldiers would face severe retaliation from their cap-

tors, and so there was a general reluctance by the War Department to allow then to fight. Indeed, the emancipation and the enlistment of blacks into service in the Union army prompted a fierce response among Southern leaders.

Within the Confederate army, calls were made to develop a "no-prisoners" policy, and many black soldiers who were captured were summarily executed. White officers who had led black regiments were often held in prisons reserved for enlisted prisoners of war, rather than the slightly better prisons for officers. As a result, abolitionist officers serving with black enlisted men frequently found themselves languishing at Andersonville, in Georgia. The result was a complete breakdown of previous agreements regarding prisoner exchanges between the Union and the Confederacy that led to the unnecessary deaths of men imprisoned by both sides.

Black soldiers and their white officers did face severe dangers in combat with revenge-seeking Confederates. In one well-documented incident, General Nathan Bedford Forrest's men destroyed Fort Pillow on the Mississippi River and executed several dozen black captives along with some white officers, including the unit's commander, Major William F. Bradford. These unfortunate soldiers were shot as they allegedly attempted to escape.

Despite the terrible risk, many African American men actively fought through the war and some, like the 54th Massachusetts, became legendary for their actions while under fire. Yet not all the black soldiers who fought in the Civil War fought for the Union.

African Americans were also found serving in the Confederate army in roles beyond that of cook, musician, and body servant to their masters. In defending their Southern homeland, black men who served in Rebel regiments were accepted freely into fully integrated units, and they functioned as soldiers trusted by their white comrades. Unfortunately, much of their activity was not recorded in the history books. The South had reasons to avoid the acknowledgment that former slaves and free black men were fighting as well as their white companions. And in the postwar North, there was little interest in recording the facts surrounding black men who fought openly against the very forces that were trying to bring equality and freedom to them. As a result, much of this fascinating glimpse into an alternative history has been denied to current generations.

There is evidence that black men served as private combat soldiers in regular Confederate regiments. For example, there is an excellent account of a black man, "one of the colored boys," who served in the 8th Virginia Cavalry Regiment, swam across a river during the battle of Stones River, Tennessee, and captured a white

The festive ceremony during the presentation of the regimental colors to the 20th United States Colored Infantry, in Union Square, New York City, on March 5, 1864. This regiment consisted of New York blacks who, ironically, had been targets of abuse and violence by white New Yorkers during the New York City draft riots less than a year before.

Troops of the 26th United States Colored Infantry on parade at Camp William, Pennsylvania. The 26th United States Colored Infantry fought in a number of skirmishes in the swamps, salt marshes, and dense forests of South Carolina in 1864.

Union sergeant. When the prisoner was delivered across the river to Confederate headquarters, he asked General "Grumble" Jones the question, "What are you going to do with me?" Jones answered, "He captured you, and now you belong to him!" The sergeant reportedly broke down in tears at General Jones' joke.

Other surviving evidence includes a Cincinnati, Ohio, newspaper account of a black soldier killed in a raid in the vicinity of Lewisburg, West Virginia. The newspaper's correspondent—a soldier who had participated in the Battle of Droop Mountain—reported that one of the first dead Confederates he had

seen as he charged across the Confederate defenses was a black man wearing a gray uniform, clutching the musket and cartridge box he had been using in an attempt to repulse the Federal attack.

Vital contributions were made by African Americans to the war efforts on both sides during the Civil War. Like the other soldiers, they served in areas of extreme hardship and danger. Yet they did so without equal pay, at first, and while enduring reports of the lynchings of other black men in New York during the draft riots of the summer of 1863. Nevertheless, they continued to serve until the end of the war the nation that had once

held them as slaves. A number of black soldiers were awarded the Congressional Medal of Honor for their extreme bravery under fire and, without a doubt, many others would have earned equal distinctions but were denied them because of the racism of the time. Generally, their war record was enviable, and the South would have done well with the early enlistment of slaves in exchange for their freedom at the end of hostilities. Unwilling to do this, the Confederacy was denied a large, and probably willing, manpower pool that might have made a profound difference in the outcome of the Civil War.

SLAVERY
The Peculiar Institution

> "Colored men were good enough to fight under Washington.... They were good enough to fight under Andrew Jackson.... They were good enough to help win American independence."
>
> —Frederick Douglass

At the time of the Civil War, the institution of slavery in America was older than the United States itself. From the beginning, slavery was a social dilemma and paradox for the American republic, which had been established on the premise that "all men are created equal." Of course, the historical roots of slavery lay not in America, but in the cultures of the ancient world. In fact, slavery has existed since the earliest days of recorded history, and slavery had been a part of African life centuries before the discovery of America.

Not long after their arrival in the New World, Europeans brought slavery, and enslaved Africans, across the Atlantic Ocean. The Americas had to be conquered and tamed, and this would require forced labor. Native Americans proved an unsuitable labor force, and the English people living in America gradually embraced faraway West Africa as a source of permanent labor. Indeed, the English colonists viewed trans-planted blacks as a solution to a host of long-standing labor-related problems that seemed insoluble in the harsh, unforgiving land that was their new home. One temporary solution, indentured servants, proved unsuccessful because it did not provide a permanent labor force. For the English colonists, African slaves provided the stable labor resource necessary to tame a virgin land of boundless potential.

Therefore, slavery in the United States was not so much a created institution as it was an inherited one. However, it was adopted by the Founding Fathers in order to ensure that Southern states would join with Northern states as one nation after the American Revolution. For this reason, among others, the institution of slavery thrived in the world's greatest democracy. Indeed, the United States was to become the largest slave-owning nation in the Western world during the antebellum period. But the American nation was destined to pay a high

TO BE SOLD on board the Ship *Bance-Island*, on tuesday the 6th of *May* next, at *Ashley-Ferry*; a choice cargo of about 250 fine healthy NEGROES, just arrived from the Windward & Rice Coast.—The utmost care has already been taken, and shall be continued, to keep them free from the least danger of being infected with the SMALL-POX, no boat having been on board, and all other communication with people from *Charles-Town* prevented. *Austin, Laurens, & Appleby.*

N. B. Full one Half of the above Negroes have had the SMALL-POX in their own Country.

PAGE 15: The headquarters of the slave trading firm of Price, Birch & Co. in Alexandria, Virginia, in August 1863. Along with other slave-trading establishments, the firm of Price, Birch & Co. thrived during the antebellum period, receiving cargoes of slaves who had survived the horrors of the Middle Passage across the Atlantic. ABOVE: A Southern newspaper advertisement by the slave-trading dealership of Austin, Laurens, & Appleby announcing the arrival of African American slaves to the thirteen colonies. The dealers were careful to assure prospective buyers that the slaves were healthy and not contaminated by smallpox.

price for clinging to an obsolete institution that mocked the meaning of freedom. This fundamental paradox of the American republic was one of the major factors that would eventually lead the nation into its most tragic upheaval: the Civil War.

African peoples from the vibrant and ancient civilizations of West Africa, primarily from the coastal lands stretching between present-day Senegal and Angola, became the slaves of the New World. The first slaves to be brought to the American colonies, some twenty Africans, disembarked from a Dutch slave ship anchored in the Chesapeake Bay, at the English colony of Jamestown, Virginia,

in 1619. Most of the slaves who were brought to America were captured in the course of tribal warfare or had been kidnapped by black and Arab slave catchers who sold them to European slave traders.

After the ordeal of capture, the slaves endured the nightmarish passage across the Atlantic in European or American cargo ships that resembled floating prisons. Many died during the difficult journey across thousands of miles of ocean. Those who survived this hell never forgot its horrors. One shocked slave, Olaudah Equiano of the Ibo tribe, believed that he "had gotten into a world of bad spirits and that [the whites] were going to kill me." He also thought that the African slaves were fated "to be eaten by those white men with horrible looks, red faces, and loose hair."

Another African, who would soon carry the slave name Charles Ball, described the surreal horror of being stolen away from his people and taken from his homeland, only to be thrown into a slave ship bound for America:

At the time we came into this [slave] ship, she was full of black people, who were all confined in a dark and low place in irons. The women were in irons as well as the men. About twenty persons were seized in our village . . . the weather was very hot whilst we lay in the river and many of us died every day.

Defiance was not unknown during the long and arduous journey across the Atlantic, which was known as the Middle Passage. Mutinies occasionally erupted on the high seas as the slaves made desperate bids for freedom, rebelling despite the slim chances for success. They refused to accept a life of bondage and were willing to die rather than serve as slaves in the New World.

Those who survived the Middle Passage were sold like cattle on the auction block. Humiliated foreigners in a strange land far from home, they were sold before large crowds of buyers. In a slave's lifetime, he or she might be sold several times. Owners would sell slaves because of excessive debt or to raise cash. Hence, most slaves in America knew more than one plantation and worked for various owners in their lifetime. Such instability was devastating to the already fragile structure of the slave family. As property, a slave—man, woman, or child—could be sold simply on the owner's whim, causing permanent breakups of black families with little or no warning. Even infants were sometimes taken from mothers and sold on the auction block. One slave described the anguish of the experience of the auction block as follows:

I was about twelve or fourteen years old when I was sold. A Negro trader came along and bought up all the slaves he could and took us to Louisiana....I was a boy then big enough to work. I had a brother named John and a cousin by the name of Brutus. Both of them were sold and about three weeks later, it came my turn. On the day I left home, everything was sad among the slaves. My mother and father sang and prayed over me and told me how to get along in the world. I took my little bundle of clothes—a pair of slips, a shirt and a pair of jean pants—and went to give my mamma my last farewell . . . when selling time came [at the Atlantic Ocean port of Charleston, South Carolina] we had to wash up and comb our hair so as to look as good as we could so as to demand a high price [and] we had to dress up and parade before the white folks until they picked the ones they

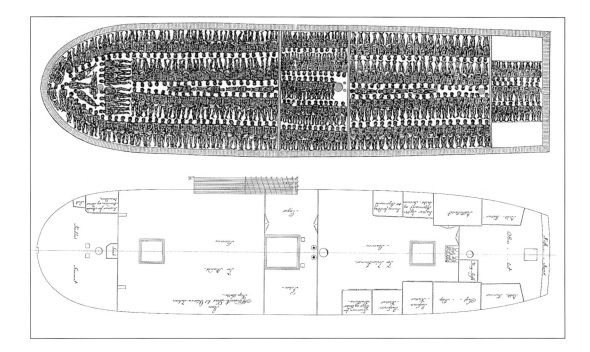

N. B. FOREST,
DEALER IN SLAVES,
No. 87 Adams-st, Memphis, Ten.,

HAS just received from North Carolina, twenty-five likely young negroes, to which he desires to call the attention of purchasers. He will be in the regular receipt of negroes from North and South Carolina every month. His Negro Depot is one of the most complete and commodious establishments of the kind in the Southern country, and his regulations exact and systematic, cleanliness, neatness and comfort being strictly observed and enforced. His aim is to furnish to customers A. 1 servants 'and field hands, sound and perfect in body and mind. Negroes taken on commission.   jan21

TOP: The carefully arranged inhuman confinement of hundreds of Africans in the infernal holds of the slave ships to maximize the number of people that could be crammed below decks for shipment to the Americas. BOTTOM: An antebellum advertisement from Memphis, Tennessee, slave trader and future Confederate general Nathan B. Forrest, who became wealthy before the war by selling slaves. General Forrest commanded the Confederate forces during the infamous Fort Pillow massacre.

wanted. I was sold along with a gang of others to a trader and he took us to Louisiana [and] out of seventeen of us sold to [the new master], only four of us got back home [after the Civil War because] some died, others he killed....

The auction block epitomized the horror of slavery, for that was where so many black families in America were shattered forever. When he was only around five or six years old, Josiah Henson endured the bitter experience of the auction block. He later described the nightmare of that ordeal: "My brothers and sisters were bid off first, and one by one, while my mother, paralyzed with grief, held me by the hand. Her turn came and she was bought." And Linda Brent, who wrote *Incidents in the Life of a Slave Girl,* which was published in 1861, described with horror how "notwithstanding my grandmother's long and faithful service to her owners, not one of her children escaped the auction block. These God-breathing machines are no more, in the sight of their masters, than the cotton they plant, or the horses they tend."

After sale at the auction block, slaves were often taken to another area or a different state. Here, the West Africans labored for a lifetime in the fields of small farmers and big planters for neither gain nor reward. In these fields of sorrow, the transplanted Africans often suffered the lash and the wrath of vengeful overseers and masters, especially while toiling on the large cotton and rice plantations of the Deep South. The great Frederick Douglass, later known as the "Sage of Anacostia" (for his District of Columbia home), described the drudgery of the average slave's life in the sprawling cotton, rice, corn, and hemp fields across the South:

We worked in all weathers. It was never too hot or too cold; it could never

The great black abolitionist from southern Maryland Frederick Douglass was the son of a white master and a slave woman. He was one of the leading voices for black equality and for the use of black troops in the Civil War.

rain, blow, hail, or snow too hard for us to work in the field. Work, work, work, was scarcely more the order of the day than of the night. The longest days were too short for him, and the shortest nights too long for him.

Despite the instability and brutality of slave life in America, and despite the plague of broken black families, an energetic African American community life not only endured, but flourished. Indeed, a rich culture thrived from sundown to sunup. During this time away from the fields and the drudgery of menial labor, the slaves created a rich social life to compensate for the brutality of slavery and to cope and survive in a harsh system. African Americans maintained a vigorous family and cultural life beyond the eyes of the white masters and the white world. They kept alive various aspects of West African life in defiance of their owners, preserving cultural ties to West Africa through music, the telling of folktales, dancing, and language patterns, magic, and beliefs. During the antebellum period, even the burials of slaves in the South were often performed according to the customs of their faraway West African homeland. In this way, the slaves maintained their dignity, personal pride, and self-esteem for generation after generation, despite their sufferings.

These transplanted Africans also turned to Christianity for spiritual strength to endure the horrors of slavery. The slaves of the New World successfully utilized those aspects of the white man's religion that inspired hope and helped them to cope with their oppressive situation. They readily identified with the plight of the Hebrew people, who had suffered as the slaves of the Egyptians, and the Old Testament stories that described their heroic struggles for freedom, perseverance and courage, and their eventual deliverance from bondage. Religion served as a source of inspiration, instilling faith and hope for a new day of freedom in the future.

While self-serving white preachers taught a controlling brand of religion that emphasized strict obedience to authority and justified slavery, black preachers rose as fiery leaders in the slave community. These African American men of God preached a religion of hope, which often sparked defiance. Forsaking the "white man's religion" was in itself an act of defiance for slaves. Hence, black religion served as a means of resisting the dehumanizing aspects of slavery while strengthening hope.

Music, another spiritual refuge, was vital to the preservation of the slaves' individuality, spirituality, and dignity. Music provided a psychological buffer and a measure of independence for slaves within the context of their bondage. The intricate rhythms of the music of West Africa were preserved for generations, becoming a permanent feature of life in African American culture. The sounds of African musical instruments, such as drums, horns, whistles, and flutes, mingled with the music of Southern culture to produce a distinctive blend that was uniquely African American. Slaves were also able to express a subtle defiance through their music with lyrics that poked fun at the master and his family or praised black cunning.

Another trait that survived among the African Americans in the New World was a defiant fighting spirit. Indeed, out of the grim conditions of the institution of slavery sprang the heroics of black resistance. The leaders of slave resistance were often the spiritual leaders of the slave community. Black ministers preached a fiery brand of spiritual liberation, which inspired resistance against masters and promoted physical liberation. The fighting prowess of African Americans had been demonstrated long before the Civil War, and the spirit of defiance and resistance continued to thrive in African American communities in the South throughout the antebellum period, manifesting itself often and in many ways.

The fighting spirit of African Americans had also been demonstrated as early as the French and Indian War, and in the American Revolution, one in five Colonial soldiers was of African descent. In fact, the first Colonial victim of British bullets during the Revolution was a runaway slave from Boston, Crispus Attucks. He was one of five patriot martyrs killed during the infamous Boston Massacre on March 5, 1770, and one of the first Americans to die for his country in its struggle for independence. This first violent clash between the British and the colonists helped to spark the revolution. And during the American Revolution, one of the first black volunteer companies was appropriately named the Attucks Company.

ABOVE: The Boston Massacre on March 5, 1770, which helped to spark the American Revolution. Among the first victims of British bullets was Crispus Attucks, a runaway slave who was mortally wounded in the initial volley. In this illustration, Attucks is seen wounded on the ground and being assisted by another colonist. RIGHT: Attucks became an early martyr of the American Revolution and his death was widely publicized in this famous handbill.

AMERICANS!
BEAR IN REMEMBRANCE
The HORRID MASSACRE!
Perpetrated in King-ftreet, BOSTON,
New-England,
On the Evening of March the Fifth, 1770.
When FIVE of your fellow countrymen,
GRAY, MAVERICK, CALDWELL, ATTUCKS,
and CARR,
Lay wallowing in their Gore!
Being *bofely*, and moft *inhumanly*
MURDERED!
And SIX others badly WOUNDED!
By a Party of the XXIXth Regiment,
Under the command of Capt. Tho. Preston.
REMEMBER!
That Two of the MURDERERS
Were convicted of MANSLAUGHTER!
By a Jury, of whom I fhall fay
NOTHING,
Branded in the hand!
And *difmiffed*,
The others were ACQUITTED,
And their Captain PENSIONED!
Alfo,
BEAR IN REMEMBRANCE
That on the 22d Day of February, 1770
The infamous
EBENEZER RICHARDSON, Informer,
And tool to Minifterial hirelings,
Moft *barbaroufly*
MURDERED
CHRISTOPHER SEIDER,
An innocent youth!
Of which crime he was found guilty
By his Country
On Friday April 20th, 1770;
But remained *Unfentenced*
On Saturday the 22d Day of February, 1772.
When the GRAND INQUEST
For Suffolk county,
Were informed, at requeft,
By the Judges of the Superior Court,
That EBENEZER RICHARDSON's *Cafe*
Then lay before his MAJESTY.
Therefore faid *Richardfon*
This day, MARCH FIFTH! 1772,
Remains UNHANGED!!!
Let THESE things be told to Pofterity!
And handed down
From Generation to Generation,
'Till Time fhall be no more!
Forever may AMERICA be preferved,
From weak and wicked monarchs,
Tyrannical Minifters,
Abandoned Governors,
Their Underlings and Hirelings!
And may the
Machinations of artful, *defigning* wretches,
Who would ENSLAVE THIS People,
Come to an end,
Let their NAMES and MEMORIES
Be buried in eternal oblivion,
And the PRESS,
For a *SCOURGE* to Tyrannical Rulers,
Remain FREE.

Both Northern and Southern blacks played prominent roles throughout the long struggle of the American Revolution. African Americans fought in virtually every battle against what was then the most powerful nation in the world, Great Britain. Prince Estabrook, a runaway slave serving in Captain John Parker's Massachusetts militia company, was among the defiant militiamen who fired the famous "shot heard around the world" at Lexington Green, Massachusetts. Other courageous black soldiers, with slave

ABOVE LEFT: *As the crack British regulars gained the fortifications of Breed's Hill during the Battle of Bunker Hill in June 1775—after most of the colonists' powder and ammunition was exhausted—Peter Salem stood firm. With his trusty flintlock, Salem then killed Major John Pitcairn, who was encouraging his Redcoats over the parapet.* **ABOVE RIGHT:** *James Lafayette and the Marquis de Lafayette, of France, worked with George Washington to aid the rebellious colonies in the American Revolution. James Lafayette—pictured posing as the Marquis' body servant at Yorktown, Virginia—worked as a double agent, gathering intelligence from the British, and may have been the first black spy to serve the new nation.*

names like Pompey, Cato Wood, Cuff Whittemore, and Peter Salem, served side by side with defiant white patriots at Concord Bridge. Along with white militiamen, these black warriors from Massachusetts stood up to the British regulars and defeated them in the second battle of the American Revolution, at Concord Bridge. And, when the lengthy attack formations of the disciplined British swarmed up Breed's Hill during the Battle of Bunker Hill outside Boston in June 1775, Peter Salem stood tall. The African American sharpshooter killed the British Major John Pitcairn, who had leaped atop the parapet to encourage the Redcoats up the hill and over the fortifications.

Throughout the American Revolution, African Americans fought beside white sol-diers in both militia and regular units. Before the war's end, the New England regiments of General George Washington's army would be filled with hundreds of black soldiers. These African Americans fought primarily in inte-grated units, which saw distinguished service throughout the American Revolution.

Nonetheless, white colonists from the South often viewed black soldiers more as a threat than as invaluable allies who could help win independence for the thirteen colonies. While some Continental units from the South contained black soldiers wearing the blue uniform of Washington's crack troops (one African American family from Virginia sent nine sons to the front), American racism drove thousands of Southern blacks to fight in the red uniforms of the British. The English promised African Americans the long-sought dream of liberty and equality if they took up arms against the colonists. That many did so was not surpris-ing since slavery was legal in every colony, even in the North. Consequently, many "British" African Americans also went into battle to defend their newly acquired free-dom with the inspiring words of liberation "Liberty to Slaves" written across their breasts.

As would be true in the Civil War, the enlistment of black troops in Colonial units was slow in coming. But by the end of 1776, enthusiasm for the war among the rebellious colonists began to wane as repeated military setbacks forced the realization that this would be a long and costly conflict. Consequently, more official efforts were initi-

ated to recruit black soldiers to fight against the British invader. By 1777 eager African Americans were recruited to fill the ranks of New England regiments, which whites were increasingly hesitant to join. Soon, thousands of African Americans, mostly from the New England colonies, were fighting for American independence during the Revolution.

Contrary to common stereotypes, the majority of blacks served not in ragtag militia outfits, but in Washington's elite Continental regiments. One white soldier in central Massachusetts described the extent of black participation in Continental regiments, noting with surprise how "no regiment [was] without a lot of Negroes" in its ranks. The number of black soldiers was especially high in the reliable and hard-fighting Continental regiments from the colonies of Maryland and Rhode Island. These hardy Continental soldiers served as the dependable shock troops of Washington's Revolutionary Army, often leading attacks or covering withdrawals during the most severe crises on the battlefield. In battle after battle, the hardy Continentals earned their reputation as Washington's finest and sturdiest troops.

The 1st Rhode Island Regiment was one of the first Colonial units to enlist black soldiers during the Revolutionary War. When the regiment was organized, the Rhode Islanders' ranks contained ninety-six former slaves and thirty free blacks. By 1778 a total of 755 African Americans were serving faithfully in various regiments of Washington's Revolutionary Army. Hardly believing his eyes, one shocked French officer, the

The tenacious defense of Breed's Hill, outside Boston, Massachusetts, at the Battle of Bunker Hill. In this illustration, a black patriot is seen in the process of replacing a flint on his musket for yet another shot at the hated English during the bitter hand-to-hand fighting inside the redoubt after the British poured over the parapet.

General Andrew Jackson's victory at Chalmette during the Battle of New Orleans in the War of 1812. Here, in January 1815, hundreds of black soldiers from New Orleans helped to repulse the attacking British in one of the most one-sided victories in American military history.

Marquis de Chastellux, wrote near the war's end how at a "ferry-crossing I met with a detachment of the Rhode Island regiment… the majority of the enlisted men are Negroes or mulattos; but they are strong, robust men, and those I saw made a good appearance." One impressed soldier witnessed the complex maneuvers of a well-trained black battalion, which would later become part of the 4th Connecticut Infantry, and described how he "saw a battalion of them, as fine, martial-looking men as I ever saw…."

Another high-ranking French officer, the Baron von Closen, who was General de Rochambeau's aide-de-camp, described the victory review at Yorktown, Virginia, noting that "three-quarters of the Rhode Island regiment consists of Negroes, and that regiment is the most neatly dressed, the best under arms, and the most precise in its maneuvers."

Such lofty praise for the discipline and fighting prowess of the African American troops was seldom forthcoming from Southerners, however.

Nevertheless, black Americans fought with distinction aboard the warships of the Continental navy, crossed the Delaware River with General Washington to win a surprising winter victory at Trenton, endured the frigid rigors of the winter encampment at snowy Valley Forge, and fought in almost every engagement of the Revolution. Black Colonial troops played a key role in helping to win the nation's independence from beginning to end. In total, as many as ten thousand black soldiers served under arms during the trying years of the American Revolution. Unfortunately, the important role of black participation during the most difficult years of the struggle for independence

has generally been underestimated and over-looked by historians.

Not surprisingly, therefore, the contributions and sacrifices of black soldiers during the American Revolution were mostly in vain. Equality, freedom, and respect were not won by the African American warriors who had struggled successfully for their nation's independence. Some black soldiers were even returned to slavery after serving for years in the conflict that won independence for the colonies. While the colonies gained their freedom from Britain, African Americans remained in bondage. Despite the idealistic words of Thomas Jefferson's Declaration of Independence, the new American nation yet retained the "peculiar institution" that it had inherited from the mother country. The colonists had rebelled against becoming the "slaves" of the British, but such idealistic revolutionary analogies were forgotten by the winners—at least in regard to African Americans—once independence was achieved.

Nevertheless, black heroics on the field of battle continued unabated in every American war after the American Revolution. The greatest one-sided victory of the War of 1812—Chalmette, or the battle of New Orleans, which propelled General Andrew Jackson to the White House—was won with the help of hundreds of black soldiers. During that crisis, General Jackson, a Southerner, placed considerable faith in the fighting prowess of the well-trained free black militiamen of New Orleans. Despite opposition, Jackson was determined that these loyal African Americans would be on his side against the might of the British invader.

Consequently, General Jackson enthusiastically rearmed the black soldiers of Louisiana. When he needed every man to defend New Orleans against the invading British army, he received the invaluable services of two black battalions and other black

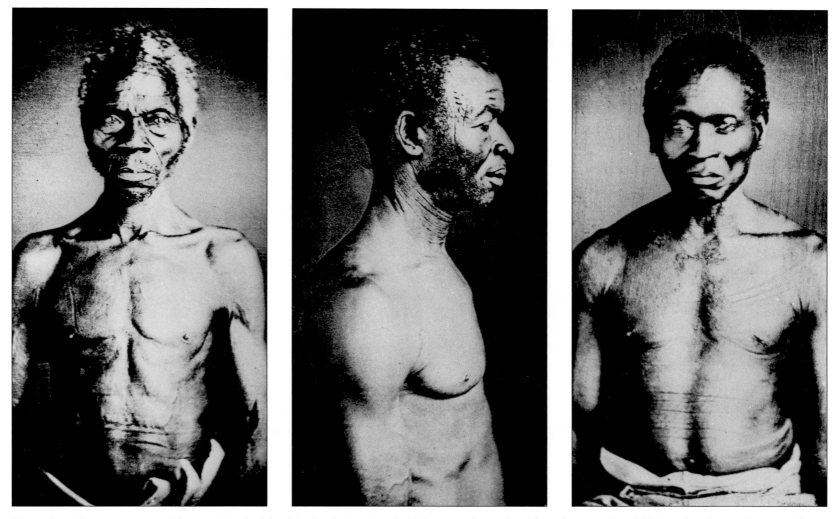

These three daguerreotypes of slaves, taken in Columbia, South Carolina, in 1850, are perhaps the oldest photographs of African Americans; they were discovered in the basement of a Harvard University museum in 1976. Pictured, from left to right, are an African American named Renty, identified as a Congo slave and listed as a slave driver on Benjamin Franklin Taylor's plantation, Edgehill; Jack, from the Guinea Coast, who is marked with decorative ritual scars on his cheek; and an unidentified man.

militia companies. On January 8, 1815, hundreds of African Americans of the Louisiana Free Men of Color and the San Domingo Free Men of Color stood firm behind the cotton-bale and mud defenses of Chalmette to repel the British attackers. Jackson claimed that the British commander at Chalmette, Sir Edward Michael Pakenham, was killed by a shot fired by one of the black rifleman from New Orleans.

During the Seminole Wars, African Americans fought against the United States in a role that has been all but forgotten. Throughout the early 1800s, slaves escaped their Georgia and Florida masters to join the Seminole, themselves eighteenth-century refugees from Georgia and Alabama, in the untamed wilderness of Florida. These self-liberated African Americans intermingled with the Seminole to become a distinctive

people, the Black-Seminoles, in a unique blending of Native American, African American, and African cultures. In the 1830s and 1840s, former slaves, Seminole, and Black-Seminole peoples formed a determined resistance that frustrated the best efforts of the U.S. military.

During the Battle of Lake Okeechobee on Christmas Day, 1837, for example, a formidable band of Seminoles, former slaves, and Black-Seminoles inflicted some of the highest casualties ever suffered by U.S. troops during an Indian war. Generally overlooked, the key participation of former slaves during the Seminole Wars was so widespread during the long years of bitter conflict in Florida that one shocked general, Sidney T. Jesup, declared that the conflict was in reality a "Negro war." Indeed, Jesup declared with surprise that "the negroes [were] the most active and determined warriors" among the elusive Seminole.

During the Mexican War of 1846–47, a company of Missouri blacks, officers' servants, was armed and organized by Colonel Alexander Doniphan. In a saga inspired by Manifest Destiny, this small unit of Missourians embarked on the longest expedition in American military history. In February 1847, the company fought in the Battle of Sacramento, in northern Mexico, which

ABOVE: The capture of Nat Turner, the fiery revolutionary and holy man who led a bloody revolt in Tidewater, Virginia, that was quickly crushed during the summer of 1831. After the insurrection was suppressed and he had hidden in the forests of Southampton County, Turner was captured by a farmer. Following a swift trial, he was hanged. RIGHT: The slave-trading establishment of Price & Burch in Alexandria, Virginia.

resulted in the American capture of Chihuahua, Mexico.

When there were no wars to fight, Southern slaves resisted the institution of slavery in many ways. Most often, slave resistance to the "peculiar institution" took the subtle forms of sabotage, apathy, or non-compliance. But large-scale, organized resistance was not unknown in the South before the Civil War. Slave revolts were actually more common in the antebellum period than during the Civil War, when there were no large uprisings, despite the invasion of the South by Union armies.

In South Carolina in 1739, more than a quarter-century before the American Revolution, the Stono Rebellion, led by a slave named Cato, resulted in the deaths of more than sixty people, both black and white. In 1800, a well-organized, ambitious plan by twenty-four-year-old Gabriel Prosser, which called for thousands of slaves to rise up in revolt in and around Richmond, Virginia, was discovered before it was launched. But in 1822 Denmark Vesey, a black carpenter born in the West Indies who bought his freedom after winning a local lottery, led a large-scale revolt in Charleston, South Carolina, with as many as nine thousand slaves. Vesey was defeated and captured, however, and hanged along with thirty-four followers. Lesser slave revolts occurred across the South from Texas to Virginia during the antebellum period; all were swiftly quelled.

The most successful slave revolt in America was led by Nat Turner, a respected black preacher from southeast Virginia, in 1831. The Virginia tidewater of Southampton County was ravaged by Turner's revolutionaries during a bloody August that the entire

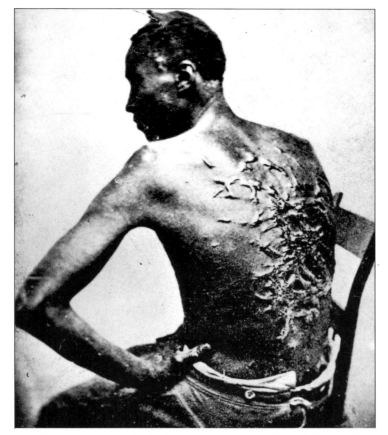

Few images more convincingly document the cruelties of slavery than this photograph, taken on April 2, 1863. This man bears the scars of severe whippings at the hands of his owner, Captain John Lyon, on Lyon's cotton plantation near Washington, Louisiana.

South would never forget. Nearly sixty whites were killed before Nat Turner and fewer than a hundred of his rebels were captured, and the revolt was crushed. Mass executions of the black rebels followed their capture. The slave prophet Turner was sent to the gallows to prevent the "infection" of slave revolt from spreading across the South.

It was no coincidence that Nat Turner, a holy man from tidewater Virginia, was the leader of the most successful slave insurrection in American history. Indeed, African Americans saw a vengeful righteousness and redemption in revolt, which they believed was sanctioned by God in the Bible. Slave preachers preached a fiery mixture of religion and liberation against the oppressors. Black holy men like Vesey and Turner implored their followers to believe that God would deliver them from bondage just as the children of Israel had been liberated from the shackles of the Egyptians. To blacks in bondage, rebellion was a holy and righteous crusade against their oppressors.

Contrary to the stereotypical and mythical "Sambo" image of the docile slave of the South, discontent and rebelliousness was widespread among African Americans across the South during the antebellum period. In fact, the South's all-consuming fear of slave insurrection was one reason that the Southern states seceded from the Union during the winter of 1860–61. The election of President Abraham Lincoln and his Republican administration made Southerners fear that the new government would promote such slave revolts. Although they were unsuccessful, the slave revolts of the antebellum period, especially Vesey's and Turner's insurrections, played an important role in leading the nation down the bloody path to the Civil War.

The stirring record of African American valor on the battlefields of all of America's wars had amply demonstrated the courage, resiliency, and heroism of African Americans long before the Civil War. So the question of their fighting ability should not have been in question at the beginning of the Civil War. Nevertheless, before they could win widespread participation in the Civil War, black Americans first had to break down stereotypes by once again proving their worth to white Americans and the nation.

The Overlooked Contribution of Freedmen, or "Contraband"

Even before black soldiers fought in the Union army on the battlefield, a large contingent of African Americans played a role in bringing about an eventual Union victory. Around a quarter of a million free blacks, known as freedmen, or contraband, supported and assisted the Union war machine in the field across the South. These newly freed slaves played a vital role in the Union effort, serving as laborers, teamsters, cooks, nurses, woodcutters, scouts, spies, river boatmen, pioneers, artisans, blacksmiths, bridge and ship builders, and so on. During the early years of the war, before African Americans were permitted to fight for the Union, free blacks served in these important noncombat roles. Later, tens of thousands of freedmen served in noncombat roles while simultaneously their black comrades fought in the Union ranks: an all-important dual contribution.

The importance of freedmen to the Union becomes obvious from the fact that while the free states contained a population of only around 225,000 blacks, the Southern states—where Union armies liberated slaves as they advanced relentlessly southward—contained a slave population of 4 million. Throughout the war years, as the Union armies pushed deeper into Confederate territory, large numbers of slaves either escaped to join the Union forces or were liberated by the conquering Yankees.

Thousands of these newly liberated blacks flocked to Federal armies, taking noncombat positions that supported and assisted Union forces that were fighting deep in Confederate territory. This mass exodus of ex-slaves from plantations and their quick assimilation into Union

TOP RIGHT: A photograph taken by Timothy H. O'Sullivan of four generations of slaves, all born on the plantation of J. J. Smith, near Beaufort, South Carolina. BOTTOM RIGHT: The day of liberation: United States Colored Troops under General Edward Augustus Wild. Wild, a Harvard-educated Massachusetts man who raised companies of black soldiers with the support of Governor Andrew of Massachusetts, here liberates slaves from bondage during an expedition in eastern North Carolina in January 1864. Formed at New Bern, North Carolina, by General Wild, who had lost an arm at the Battle of South Mountain, these troops served with pride as members of "Wild's African Brigade."

Contrabands—fugitive slaves and slaves liberated by Union armies—marching to work at Fort Monroe on the tip of the Virginia Peninsula, southeast of Richmond, Virginia.

Contrabands relax outside a cook tent in a Union encampment at Culpeper, Virginia, during November 1863, in this photograph by Timothy H. O'Sullivan.

armies translated into an important equation that would play a large part in determining winner from loser during a lengthy and bloody war of attrition. Indeed, the freedmen flooding into Federal armies by the thousands to take noncombat roles meant that more Union fighting men could now serve on the firing line instead of being assigned to rear-guard duties.

In this way, thousands of ex-slaves concretely served the Union long before the first African American soldiers donned blue uniforms. But perhaps as important in terms of the overall success of the Union war effort, the thousands of newly liberated slaves who flocked into the Union armies denied the manpower-short Confederacy what it needed most of all to survive and win its war of attrition against the more powerful North: its "invisible" armies of slaves who had supported and assisted Southern armies in the field, allowing more Rebel soldiers to fight on the front.

TOP: Contrabands on the South Carolina plantation of General Thomas F. Drayton, a West Pointer who served as a brigade commander in General Robert E. Lee's Army of Northern Virginia during the Maryland campaign, after the plantation's occupation by Union troops. LEFT: In a contraband encampment at City Point, Virginia, a primary supply base for the Army of the Potomac during its campaigns in Virginia, a man of God preaches to men, women, and children who were once slaves. Religion was one of the few public practices that allowed African Americans a measure of community, authority, and self-expression. Many, both free and in bondage, found strength and hope in the exercise of their faith.

chapter

2

1862–1863:
The Call to Arms

Quite simply, without African Americans—who composed twelve percent of the Union's armed forces—the North would not have won the Civil War. By the end of bloody 1862, and after almost two years of bitter fighting, the Union was losing the war. Horrendous losses, the elusiveness of decisive victory, and a series of battlefield defeats like the one at Fredericksburg, Virginia, in December 1862, caused a war-weariness to spread across the North. Increasingly, Northerners contemplated allowing the South to exist as an independent nation just to halt the bloodletting, which seemed as if it would never end. A negotiated peace was beginning to seem like the only recourse to many people across the North.

The fratricidal conflict had become a bloody war of attrition. During only the first two years of war, the slaughter of the battles of Shiloh, the Seven Days, the Second Bull Run, Antietam, and Stones River had shocked both sides into a new realization of the terrible cost of this conflict. It seemed as if the

endless killing might continue for years, punishing both the Union and the Confederacy for their folly.

With a population more than double that of the South—there were twenty-two million Northerners versus nine million Southerners—the North could expect to endure and survive longer in a war of attrition than the resource-short Confederacy. Nevertheless, an ever-increasing war-weariness—the weakness of a democracy during a lengthy and costly war—was seemingly leading the North toward a negotiated peace settlement instead of a decisive victory. Because President Lincoln's war effort no longer enjoyed the limitless and enthusiastic support of the people, the Northern war machine faced a serious manpower crisis by late 1862. No longer were tens of thousands of Northern volunteers rushing forth eagerly to enlist to fulfill President Lincoln's sacred goal of saving the Union.

By the end of 1862, therefore, the North's dwindling manpower pool had to be supplemented if this exhausting war was going to realize President Lincoln's dream of reuniting

> *"The colored population is the great available and yet unavailed of force for restoring the Union. The bare sight of fifty thousand armed and drilled black soldiers upon the banks of the Mississippi would end the rebellion at once."*
>
> —President Abraham Lincoln

PAGE 31: Black enlisted men, along with a drummer boy and a white officer, in formation at Camp William Penn, Pennsylvania. Based on a photograph, this famous painting, titled "Come Join Us, Brothers," was used on recruiting posters, which encouraged enlistment of blacks in Chicago, Illinois, in 1863. ABOVE: In order to evade the unpopular draft and to compensate for the reduced enthusiasm for the war that resulted from battlefield defeats and the length and cost of the conflict, some wealthy Northern whites hired black substitutes to take their place in the ranks. In this illustration, a black substitute enlists in the Union army.

victory on the battlefield. For African Americans, the war involved a struggle against the odds on two fronts. Blacks in America engaged in two struggles during the Civil War: to defeat the Rebels on the battlefield and to win equality and respect in American society for the advancement of African Americans.

The Union had been reluctant to accept the enlistment of African Americans at the war's beginning. But this dilemma was nothing new for blacks in America. Such discrimination had existed for patriotic blacks in America at an early date, beginning with the American Revolution. Throughout America's many wars, white resistance to black participation in the nation's conflicts remained as prevalent as the stirring heroism of African American soldiers.

At the beginning of the Civil War, the National Militia Act of 1792 still excluded blacks from military service. This exclusion of African Americans was upheld in 1861, in part because the war was so popular among whites at its start. The patriotic mood among Northerners ensured that the struggle to preserve the cherished Union was a "white man's war" during the optimistic days of 1861, when both Northerners and Southerners believed that a decisive victory could be won in only a few months. Thousands of white volunteers marched off to war with naive illusions of a quick and easy victory over their opponents.

Allowing African Americans to share in the glory of this righteous crusade was not seriously considered by Northern officials and leaders at the war's beginning. Even President Lincoln found reasons to hesitate to include blacks in the war effort. Ever the savvy Illinois politician, he understood the importance of the West, and wanted to keep the crucial border slave states—Missouri, Kentucky, and Maryland—solidly in the Union, especially during the early years of

the nation. The North's only hope of eventually grinding its way to decisive victory lay in a previously untapped resource: African Americans. In the South alone, more than four million African Americans lived in bondage among five million whites. The African American people were a vital resource, unrealized at the war's beginning, that was to ensure decisive victory for the North.

More than 200,000 African Americans rallied to the call, as their white countrymen had done earlier in the war. In one of her last diary entries, amid the gloom of the decisive Confederate defeat following General Robert E. Lee's surrender at Appomattox Court House, Mary Chesnut of Richmond described a key turning point in the war. Focusing on the importance of manpower, Chesnut wrote that while "we talked of negro recruits the Yankees used them—18 million against six. The odds too great."

But there was much more to African Americans' desire to fight for their country than simply wanting to help win a decisive the war. If he enlisted thousands of black troops, as the abolitionists and free blacks of the North advocated, then the border states, which were settled largely by Southerners, might decide to throw their support and their considerable manpower and resources to the Confederacy. Lincoln feared that this could tip the scales in the South's favor. So African Americans were excluded from participation in the great national struggle for survival.

Beginning with the firing of Southern cannons on Fort Sumter in Charleston, South Carolina, in April 1861 there was an avalanche of appeals from African Americans wanting to fight in the Civil War. In fact, even before the first shots of the war were fired, many free blacks who were members of abolitionist organizations in Northern cities rallied behind Lincoln. To support the Republican party, Northern blacks had

enlisted in Republican Clubs and in "Wide Awake" organizations with the great goal of abolition. With the outbreak of war, these African Americans made vigorous appeals to enlist in the armed forces.

Free blacks across the North welcomed the Civil War because this national crisis brought with it the seeds of radical change, which could only improve the plight of African Americans in the United States. Early

Dress parade and review of troops of the 1st South Carolina Volunteers at their encampment at Hilton Head, South Carolina, on June 25, 1862.

on, Frederick Douglass preached that dis-union was the only possible solution for uplifting the black race. Douglass also understood that the Union's salvation could be won only with the abolition of slavery, which could turn a civil war into a righteous crusade for freedom and equality.

To men with foresight and vision like Douglass, the conflict between the North and the South offered a long-awaited opportunity for blacks. Indeed, this was a chance for the Union to yet live up to the lofty and elusive promise of equality and freedom for all men that had been so boldly declared in the Declaration of Independence. Hence, Douglass knew that this vicious war brought the long-sought opportunity to end slavery, and he became the most vocal advocate for the enlistment of blacks during the early days of the Civil War.

With the first shot of the war fired in Charleston Harbor, African Americans across the North formed militia companies in response to the call to arms. One such militia unit—named in honor of the brilliant African general of antiquity—was the Hannibal Guards. This militia unit of zealous black volunteers from Pittsburgh rallied to fight for the Union, as did volunteer units of black soldiers from large cities across the North. Blacks in such cities as Boston, Providence, Philadelphia, and New York offered their services to the Union.

African American enthusiasm for enlistment came from the western states as well. Blacks in Cleveland pointed to a rich historical record and proudly proclaimed that "as in the times of '76, and the days of 1812, we are ready to go forth and do battle in the common cause of the country." To these patriotic—and politically astute—volunteers, direct participation in the conflict, fighting with distinction on the battlefield, was the shortest and most effective way to win equal rights as American citizens.

However, the early appeals of these dedicated African Americans fell on deaf ears. The government instantly rejected these requests. No one was more shocked by the government's apathy and folly than Douglass, who asked with undeniable logic and open disbelief, "What upon earth is the matter with the American Government and people?" In early 1862, Douglass boldly challenged the contradictions of American life, which were now permanent fixtures of American society. The great black abolitionist and former slave from the eastern border state of Maryland relied upon the impressive historical record of past accomplishments by African Americans to make the case for immediate black enlistment in Union armies.

Colored men were good enough to fight under Washington. They are not good enough to fight under [General George] McClellan. They were good enough to fight under Andrew Jackson. They are not good enough to fight under Gen. [Henry W.] Halleck. They were good enough to help win American independence, but they are not good enough to help preserve that independence against treason and rebellion.

Despite the many appeals and protests from the black community, the government's firm resistance to black enlistment changed only when the North began to lose the war. A combination of factors contributed to this sudden change in sentiment and policy: the North was trapped in a bloody stalemate

Fugitive families on the move, fording the Rappahannock River in central Virginia to escape the ravages of war and the advance of General Stonewall Jackson's forces in August 1862. Perhaps some of these African Americans were destined to serve as either contrabands or soldiers in the Union army.

"Once let the black man get upon his person the brass letters 'U.S.'; let him get an eagle on his button, and a musket on his shoulder and bullets in his pocket, and there is no power on earth which can deny that he has earned the right to citizenship."

—Frederick Douglass

with no end in sight; the Union war effort was hampered by chronic manpower shortages; tens of thousands of black refugees recently liberated by Yankee armies were a readily available and untapped manpower resource; war-weariness was reaching new heights across the North; and there was a slowdown in enlistment in Union armies. Also, President Lincoln, the master politician, was determined to do whatever was necessary to ensure that neither France, now in Mexico at the border of the Confederacy, nor Britain would recognize the Confederacy. Such recognition would have all but ensured the South's independence and a negotiated peace settlement. These political and military necessities caused Lincoln to finally decide that the time was right to issue his

Emancipation Proclamation, which claimed the moral high ground for the North by transforming the conflict into a struggle for human freedom. Neither France nor Britain could oppose such a righteous crusade.

A bloody string of Northern defeats had preceded the Union success at Antietam, which resulted in the repulse of General Robert E. Lee's invasion of Maryland. This victory made it possible for Lincoln to issue his famous proclamation without betraying the Union's desperation. Finally issued on September 22, 1862, only five days after the Union victory along Antietam Creek in western Maryland, the Emancipation Proclamation made the revolutionary promise that on January 1, 1863, all slaves in the Southern states in rebellion would be "forever free." Lincoln had reclaimed the moral high ground for the Union, while negating the legitimacy of the Confederacy's right to revolution and self-determination.

In a single stroke, the door to mass black enlistment in Union armies was opened. In the words of Lieutenant Colonel Norwood P. Hallowell, a white officer who would one day lead the 55th Massachusetts Colored Infantry, "We called upon them in the day of our trial, when volunteering had ceased, when the draft was a partial failure, and the bounty system a senseless extravagance." Lincoln was a product of the West and instinctively understood that the Mississippi Valley and River were the keys to winning the war. He emphasized the importance of the future contributions of black soldiery in the struggle to save the Union by predicting that

> *the colored population is the great available and yet unavailed of force for restoring the Union. The bare sight of fifty thousand armed and drilled black soldiers upon the banks of the Mississippi would end the rebellion at once.*

Long the most forceful black advocate for emancipation, Douglass wrote prophetically that

> *there is but one…effective way to suppress [the rebellion and] the simple way, then, to put an end to the savage and desolating war now waged by the slave holders, is to strike down slavery itself, the primary cause of that war [because] slavery is the sole support of the rebel cause [and hence] the stomach of this rebellion.*

Lieutenant William B. Sears, of Colonel Ambrose E. Burnside's 2nd Rhode Island Volunteer Infantry, posed beside his young servant, who wears a kepi. Often without family, such young African American boys were "adopted" by regiments such as the 2nd Rhode Island, which comprised a large number of New England abolitionists, humanitarians, and idealists.

Indeed, the four million slaves in the South served as the Confederacy's invisible army. Year after year, Southern slaves had kept the economic infrastructure firmly in place and functioning throughout the Confederacy, but the Emancipation Proclamation would help knock this pillar of support out from under the Southern war effort.

Thus Lincoln's famous decree was more a political and military solution than a humanitarian act. But the everlasting dream of Douglass and thousands of other free blacks across the North had been realized at last. A joyous Douglass proclaimed the fulfillment of one of his greatest desires, writing, "Let the slaves and free colored people be called into service, and formed into a liberating army, to march into the South and raise the banner of emancipation among the slaves." For African Americans, a long struggle had been waged merely to earn the right to fight for liberty.

Though freeing the slaves had been, in fact, only a secondary aim of an administration determined to win the war at any cost, the Northern war effort now began to be fueled by the ideology of freedom for blacks. Most immediately, regaining the moral high ground revitalized the North's war machine, bringing a flood of black recruits, strengthening the Union's armies in terms of both manpower and spirit. The war would be won with the help of tens of thousands of former slaves from the South and the sons and grandsons of slaves from the North. The conflict became, more than ever, a moral and righteous crusade for the Union.

Almost six months before Lincoln's Emancipation Proclamation, the first effort to recruit and arm black troops had been doomed to failure. Initiated in April 1862 by General David Hunter, an abolitionist who was in command of the coastal lands of South Carolina, Georgia, and northeastern

In this painting by Civil War artist Rick Reeves, soldiers of the 26th United States Colored Troops charge Rebels in a skirmish in South Carolina.

1862–1863: THE CALL TO ARMS

Brigadier General Rufus Saxton, an enlightened abolitionist, extensively recruited black troops along the coastal lands of South Carolina and the Sea Islands. The result was the 1st South Carolina Volunteers.

General Hunter's regiment of fugitive slaves was also to serve as the nucleus for the later organization of the first regular-army, all-black regiment. With this long-term goal in mind, when General Hunter mustered his fledgling regiment, he retained a single company. This remaining African American company served as the solid foundation for the creation of a new black regiment. One dependable soldier from the old "Hunter Regiment" who exemplified its high quality was Sergeant Prince Rivers. In the words of a white officer, Sergeant Rivers was "a natural king" among the black soldiers. Determined black warriors from the old Hunter Regiment, like Sergeant Rivers, the future regimental

color sergeant, would provide a dependable, solid cadre for the creation of a new regiment of African American soldiers from the sea islands of South Carolina.

In the fall of 1862, the new regiment officially became the 1st South Carolina Volunteers. Like Hunter's old regiment, the fledgling unit consisted primarily of African Americans from the "liberated" sea islands of South Carolina in the Beaufort area. But other black soldiers in the regiment hailed from the coastal lands of eastern Georgia and Florida, including black Catholics from St. Augustine, Florida, where African American culture had intermingled early with Hispanic culture. Starting in November 1862, Colonel Thomas

Florida, this first attempt to organize black troops resulted in the formation of the 1st South Carolina Colored Regiment. Here on the islands of South Carolina, Hunter was determined to turn fugitive slaves into Union soldiers. But Hunter's efforts, which were accompanied by his own unauthorized emancipation proclamation, were aborted before the regiment saw combat—President Lincoln feared this "experiment" would alienate the key border states. The regiment was disbanded in August 1862 after only four months of noncombat service. Nevertheless, the formation of the 1st South Carolina served as a catalyst that brought the topic of black enlistment to the top levels of government, even to President Lincoln himself. Lincoln realized then that the controversial issue of black enlistment could no longer be ignored or avoided.

Union troops fighting the Rebels in South Carolina in 1864. In this scene, the African American soldiers are attacked not only by the charging Rebel cavalry, but also by a pack of bloodhounds, which certainly brought back memories of the many risks of attempting to escape bondage by running away from plantations in the South.

Black troops, probably of the 1st South Carolina Volunteers, in formation on the parade ground at the Union encampment at Beaufort, South Carolina.

1862–1863: THE CALL TO ARMS

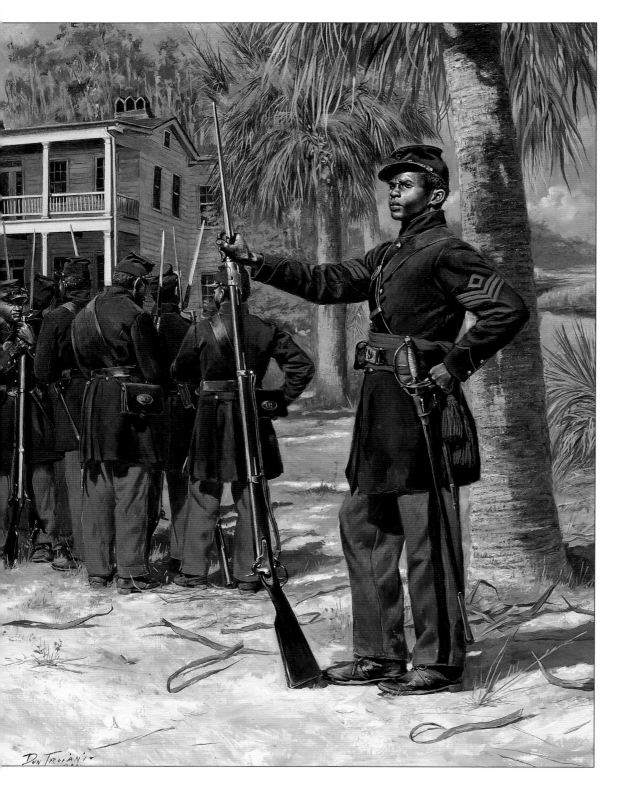

Wentworth Higginson was proud to command, in his own words, "the first slave regiment mustered into the service of the United States."

Higginson, the first commander of the first regular-army regiment of African Americans, was a thirty-seven-year-old Harvard-educated minister. An abolitionist and a fine writer from a leading New England family, Higginson was an ideal choice to command the new regiment. To him, abolition was a passion second to none, and he had been a leading force in militant antislavery activities before the war. Higginson had supported the antislavery forces in "Bloody Kansas," running guns and providing other assistance to the Kansans on the plains battleground where the sectional conflict had erupted between opposing factions during the mid-1850s to determine whether Kansas would be a free or slave state.

In addition, Higginson was an early supporter, both financially and morally, of the martyred idol John Brown. A white revolutionary, Brown had possessed the grand vision of spreading slave revolt and liberation across the South. To achieve his abolitionist goal, Brown had led the famous 1859 raid on the U.S. arsenal at Harpers Ferry, Virginia, which was to have been the spark for slave revolts across the South. However, the arrival of U.S. troops under the command of Robert E. Lee crushed Brown's revolutionaries, black and white. Like slave liberators such as Vesey and Turner, John Brown went to the gallows for his "crimes."

Higginson knew that he had much good material from which to form a new regiment of black troops. He described with admiration how "there is one company in particular,

An African American soldier on guard duty. Like the many men and women at the front or behind the lines, this soldier was fighting for the Union, and for a brighter future for blacks in America.

1862–1863: THE CALL TO ARMS

Taking the offensive, African American soldiers surge across open ground to attack Rebels who are defending their position with the advantage of natural cover.

Colonel Higginson was correct in his estimation of the combat capabilities of the black troops from South Carolina and Florida. They would soon prove that they were well-suited for offensive operations, especially the attack.

The 1st South Carolina Volunteers were successful in their early amphibious operations up Florida's St. Mary's River in early 1863, as well as in offensive operations on other Deep South waterways, such as the Edisto River. They helped to capture Jacksonville, Florida, and raise the U.S. flag over the fallen Rebel city. Afterward, striking a blow against the enemy's homeland, the St. Mary's expedition took the black soldiers deeper into Confederate territory.

By this time, the 2nd South Carolina Volunteers had also been organized. This new black regiment joined Higginson's 1st South Carolina Volunteers on the expedition into the South, where many of these men had toiled for years in the hell of slavery. For them, taking the war to the enemy was merely righteous retribution for past wrongs and injustices. Also organized from ex-slaves of the sea islands of South Carolina, the 2nd South Carolina was led by the fiery Colonel James Montgomery, a famous Jayhawke chieftain—a guerrilla fighter from Kansas who had fought proslavery Missourians for years in "Bloody Kansas" before the Civil War.

If Montgomery was consumed with righteous revenge, the New England blue-blood and moralist Higginson was not. For Colonel Higginson, the express purpose of expeditions deep into enemy country was "to carry the proclamation of freedom to the enslaved; to call all loyal men into the service of the United States [and] to occupy as much of the State of Florida as possible." The righteous work of taking the war to the Rebels was directed toward the "liberation" of slaves. Some military incursions into Florida were launched to free family

all Florida men, which I certainly think the finest-looking company I ever saw, white or black; they range admirably in size, have remarkable erectness and ease of carriage, and really march splendidly." While marching through the steamy swamps and pouring rains of South Carolina, these hardy African American soldiers, to Colonel Higginson's delight, often sang "the John Brown song." Like no other, this song inspired the African Americans to endure the rigors of campaigning with discipline and single-minded purpose.

But Higginson was most impressed by the fighting potential of the black soldiers from the Atlantic coastal lands. Early on, he worried:

Their best qualities will be wasted by merely keeping them for garrison duty. They seem peculiarly fitted for offensive operations, and especially for partisan warfare; they have so much dash and such abundant resources, combined with such an Indian-like knowledge of the country and its ways.

"No officer in this regiment now doubts that the key to the successful prosecution of the war lies in the unlimited employment of black troops."

—Colonel Thomas W. Higginson

1862–1863: The Call to Arms

members of black soldiers. Of course, these expeditions were especially appealing to the Floridian soldiers who were former slaves.

Taking the war to the enemy in the tradition of the generals William T. Sherman and Ulysses S. Grant, both Higginson's and Montgomery's black regiments conducted penetrating raids into the interiors of Georgia and Florida. Engaged in a holy war, these African American soldiers struck deep in Confederate territory, where their enemy least expected to see blacks in blue uniforms. General Hunter, who commanded the Department of the South, described the important contributions of the regiments of his department:

> *In the field these regiments, so far as tried, have proved brave, active, docile, and energetic, frequently outrunning by their zeal and familiarity with the Southern country the restrictions deemed prudent by certain of their officers and [in] so conducting themselves, upon the whole, that even our enemies, though more anxious to find fault with these than with any other portion of our troops, have not yet been able to allege against them a single violation of any of the rules of civilized warfare [and] I find the colored regiments hardy, generous, temperate, strictly obedient, possessing remarkable aptitude for military training, and deeply imbued with that religious sentiment (call it fanaticism, such as like) which made the soldiers of Oliver Cromwell invincible. They are imbued with a burning faith that now is the time appointed by God, in His All-wise Providence, for the deliverance of their race; and under the heroic incitement of this faith I believe them capable of courage and persistence of purpose which must in the end extort both victory and admiration. . . .*

Other Northern commanders readily agreed with the early views of General Hunter, who praised the virtues of the black soldiery for all to hear. Beginning in the late summer of 1862 in the faraway West, General James H. Lane was busy in Kansas with his own project of raising two black regiments. Like Colonel Montgomery, General Lane was a Kansas Jayhawker who had battled Missourians in that frontier slave state. In August 1862, even before the recruitment of Colonel Higginson's 1st South Carolina Volunteers, Lane began recruiting his Kansas regiment of black soldiers. He relied upon former slaves from neighboring Missouri and free Northern blacks to fill the ranks of his units.

Early success for blacks in Union uniforms was not long in coming. The first pitched battle in which African American troops met the Rebels was fought at Island Mounds, Missouri, in late October 1862. This little-known skirmish, which resulted in the deaths of ten members of the 1st Kansas Colored Volunteers, saw the first black combat casualties of the war. However, because this rather obscure battle was fought in a long-overlooked arena, the role of African Americans received little attention from their contemporaries and remains largely unrecognized by historians to this day.

Although not officially recognized by the War Department until early 1863, after the issuing of the Emancipation Proclamation, General Lane's African Americans of the 1st Kansas Colored Volunteers fought in skirmishes during the vicious guerrilla warfare

The Battle of Olustee, west of Jacksonville, Florida, on February 20, 1864. The 8th and 35th United States Colored Troops and 54th Massachusetts Volunteer Infantry fought in what was to be the largest battle in Florida, sometimes called the Battle of Ocean Pond.

A contraband cook in an encampment of the Army of the Potomac. Such contrabands often performed the necessary rear-echelon duties so that more veterans could fight on the front lines during a brutal war of attrition.

1862–1863: THE CALL TO ARMS

that consumed Missouri, Kansas, and the Indian Territory. These African American warriors also conducted scouting forays and reconnaissances over wide areas of the western frontier.

Thereafter the 1st Kansas Colored Volunteers continued to fight in Union blue under Colonel James M. Williams. Then the 1st Kansas Colored Volunteers officially became the 79th United States Colored Infantry. The 79th participated in none of the major battles of the war, but this fine black unit representing Kansas nonetheless compiled a distinguished record in some of the lesser-known conflicts. By the war's end, the Kansas regiment ranked twenty-first among all Union regiments in the percentage of its members who were killed in action. Part of this staggering toll was due to the Confederate policy of killing black prisoners on the battlefield. Many wounded and injured soldiers of the 1st Kansas Colored Volunteers were killed in a massacre by unmerciful Texas Rebels at Poison Springs, Arkansas, on April 18, 1864. After receiving its baptismal fire in the battle at Island Mounds, this black unit fought at Sherwood in Missouri, at Lawrence in Kansas, at Cabin Creek, Honey Springs, Fort Gibson, Baxter Springs, and Flat Rock in the Indian Territory, and at Horse Head Creek, Poison Springs, Ivy Ford, and Roseville in Arkansas.

Also, during the summer of 1862, Union General Benjamin Butler began arming blacks from African American militia units which had been organized in Louisiana at the beginning of the war. One of these militia units, the Louisiana Native Guards, which included African American officers, unlike other black units, was originally a Confederate unit. They had served in Louisiana's defense before the capture of New Orleans by the Union navy during the spring of 1862. The large free black population of New Orleans had demanded repre-

Dressed in rags, a contraband named Jackson entered a Union encampment, only to emerge as the well-uniformed drummer boy of an African American regiment, the 79th United States Colored Troops. These two popular photographs were circulated across the North to advertise the successful transformation of former slaves into Union soldiers who could defeat the Rebels on their own territory.

sentation in the military, and the Confederate government had acquiesced at an early date. After the fall of New Orleans, General Butler, a controversial Massachusetts politician, federalized these African American militia units, bringing them into Union service. Thereafter, runaway slaves swelled the ranks of Butler's black units, earning the general a reputation for infamy across the South.

Now in Union blue, the fighting men of the Louisiana Native Guards consisted of former slaves, free blacks, and Creoles of French and African heritage from southern Louisiana. So many African Americans were organized into Butler's units that they formed the 1st, 2nd and 3rd Louisiana Native Guards regiments. Though not yet officially mustered into Union service, these African American

"They are imbued with a burning faith that now is the time appointed by God, in His All-wise Providence, for the deliverance of their race; and under the heroic incitement of this faith I believe them capable of courage and persistence of purpose which must in the end extort both victory and admiration."

—General David Hunter

went out in both English and French, emphasized memories of the past glories of the black soldiers who fought with distinction under Andrew Jackson during one of the greatest crises of the War of 1812.

To Arms! It is an honor understood by our fathers who fought on the plains of Chalmette [in defense of New Orleans]. He who defends his fatherland is the real citizen, and this time we are fighting for the rights of our race....

Such emotional, patriotic appeals were effective in bringing forth hundreds of slaves from across Louisiana. By August 1863, General Banks counted almost fifteen thousand black soldiers under arms, all ready to help crush the rebellion.

The widespread employment of black troops marked a decisive turning point in the Civil War, which now became a second American revolution, fought to win equal rights for all Americans and redefine the meaning of America. Now envisioning decisive victory where none could have existed previously, the prophetic Colonel Higginson, commander of the 1st South Carolina Volunteers, reported to the War Department in Washington, D.C., with pride: "Nobody knows anything about these men who has not seen them in battle [and now] no officer in this regiment now doubts that the key to the successful prosecution of the war lies in the unlimited employment of black troops."

soldiers marched forth in November 1862, ready for action and eager to prove themselves on the field of battle.

General Nathaniel Prentiss Banks, another political general from Massachusetts, who succeeded General Butler in command of the Department of the Gulf, replaced black officers with white officers, as more African American recruits from Louisiana swelled the numbers of these units. During the spring of 1863, General Banks busily recruited his "Corps d'Afrique" from the plantations and the principal city of Louisiana: New Orleans. In this city, the appeal for recruits, which

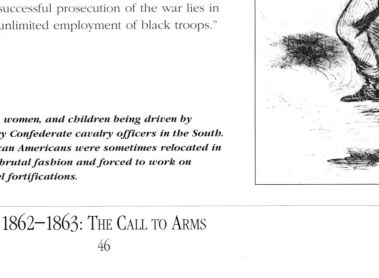

Men, women, and children being driven by angry Confederate cavalry officers in the South. African Americans were sometimes relocated in this brutal fashion and forced to work on Rebel fortifications.

1862–1863: The Call to Arms

African Americans in the Army of the James

Although it existed for only a year and a half, the Army of the James nonetheless played a key role in the Union victories at Petersburg, Virginia, and Fort Fisher, North Carolina, as well as the capture of Richmond, Virginia, and the surrender of General Robert E. Lee's Army of Northern Virginia in the final days of the war.

But the historic importance of the Army of the James lies in the fact that a larger percentage of black troops served in its ranks than in any other Northern army. Indeed, the Army of the James was the first and only Civil War army to contain an entire corps consisting of only black troops.

The success story of the African American troops of the Army of the James was in large part the result of the efforts of General Benjamin F. Butler. General Butler—detested in the South, where he was known as "Beast Butler"—was a New England liberal and enlightened humanitarian in regard to the welfare of African Americans. Indeed, he was the best friend of the black troops under his command. The pater-nalistic commander of the Army of the James, General Butler was an early advocate of black troops who stood by his strong belief in their equality to white soldiers.

General Butler, a politician from Massachusetts, demonstrated an unprecedented concern for fairness in the overall welfare of his African Americans that was rare among army commanders. He was a forceful advocate of equal treatment, and intolerant of discrimination. For instance, he demanded that his black troops possess the same quality of equipment, weaponry, medical care, and

ABOVE: *Dutch Gap on the James River, Virginia, in March 1865. Many black troops of the Army of the James served in this vicinity during the Bermuda Hundred campaign in the summer of 1864. General Ambrose E. Burnside's troops of the Army of the James, including the 4th, 6th, 10th, 36th, 38th, and 100th United States Colored Regiments, helped to construct the Dutch Gap Canal that allowed Federal gunboats to approach Richmond and attack the Confederate river defenses before Richmond.* LEFT: *General Benjamin F. Butler was an idealistic abolitionist who stood by his beliefs that black soldiers could perform as well as whites. He actively sought black soldiers, and built up a number of black regiments in the Army of the James. He was an early advocate of equal pay for African American soldiers, and demanded that they be outfitted with the same quality of equipment and weaponry as their white counterparts.* RIGHT: *Vigilant African American privates of the Army of the James on picket duty at Dutch Gap during the Bermuda Hundred campaign.*

training as white soldiers. And while other commanders used black troops in an infantry role, General Butler's Army of the James included African American artillery and cavalry units. In this sense, he proved to be more flexible in the utilization of black troops than other commanders. In total, thirty-five black units served in the Army of the James, and the majority of these regiments and batteries were obtained by General Butler's tireless efforts to secure African American soldiers.

Breaking much new ground in terms of equal and fair treatment for black soldiers, General Butler's personal commitment to the African Americans serving under him went beyond the usual concerns of an army commander. He was an early advocate of equal pay for black and white troops long before the Federal government passed the equal payment law in mid-1864. But General Butler's concerns for his African American troops went beyond the obvious need for equal pay, training, and equipment. He paid his black recruits bounties, obtained the best-qualified white officers to command his black troops, and improved sanitation and the quality of camp life. He initiated a program of missionary and relief workers to educate the ex-slaves now in uniform, established schools of learning for each African American unit, and promoted religious teachings and chose quality chaplains. He ensured that his black soldiers would be tried by United States Colored Infantry officers to ensure fair treatment at court-martial proceedings, and attempted to bargain with Confederate authorities to ensure fair treatment for captured blacks.

Beyond the battlefield, his efforts continued. He assisted the families of African American soldiers, arranging for homes

Private James Gardiner of the 36th United States Colored Troops, Army of the James. This regiment had been originally organized in late October 1862 as the 2nd North Carolina Volunteers.

First Sergeant Robert A. Pinn, 5th United States Colored Troops, Army of the James.

and employment in the North for the widows and orphans of black soldiers. He employed and assisted African Americans not in uniform with military-related jobs and established an active Office of Negro Affairs that fed, housed, and clothed thousands of black dependents. He even set up a freedman's savings bank for the financial welfare of the ex-slaves. By any measure, General

First Sergeant Powhatan Beaty, 5th United States Colored Troops, Army of the James. Private Beaty might well have been part Native American, as his first name is that of Virginia Algonquins. Most of the soldiers of the 5th United States Colored Troops hailed from Ohio.

Butler's extensive efforts not only to assist and uplift his black soldiers but also to help their families by way of equal opportunity, fair treatment, and justice were unprecedented in the military at this time.

Most of all, General Butler understood that battlefield success would be instrumental in blacks gaining a wider acceptance into American society, breaking down the prejudice

and racism of whites in the North. Unlike most army commanders, therefore, he often assigned his African American troops to the most challenging assignments on the battlefield so that they could prove themselves, and earn the respect and recognition of whites by hard fighting and battlefield success.

Consequently, the black soldiers of General Butler's Army of the James were highly motivated and high-spirited. In the words of a sergeant major of the 4th United States Colored Infantry: "A double purpose induced me and most others to enlist, to assist in abolishing slavery and to save the country from ruin." Another reason for the high spirits among the African Americans of the Army of the James was because General Butler promoted morale by designing a Medal of Valor to honor the courage of ex-slaves on the battlefield. As a measure of the widespread heroism of blacks in the battles of the Army of the James and the success of General Butler's efforts, nearly thirty African American soldiers in the Army of the James won the Congressional Medal of Honor.

An artilleryman of the 14th Rhode Island Heavy Artillery in action.

chapter 3

THE STORY OF THE 54TH MASSACHUSETTS

Glory at Fort Wagner

"One of the fiercest struggles of the war, considering the numbers engaged."

—Captain Luis F. Emilio

The attack of the 54th Massachusetts Volunteer Infantry on Fort Wagner, South Carolina, is the most famous exploit by African American troops in the Civil War. Here, more than in any other engagement during the four years of war, the combat capabilities and fighting prowess of black Union troops finally won full recognition from the American pubic.

The story of the 54th Massachusetts is a tale of glory. But it's an account of glory won for a larger purpose: the shattering of racist stereotypes and the acceptance of the black man as the equal of whites on the battlefield. This Massachusetts infantry unit was the first regiment of free blacks to be recruited in the North and the most famous of the 166 black Civil War regiments. The 54th Massachusetts was organized after Lincoln's Emancipation Proclamation as a result of the tireless efforts of the abolitionist Massachusetts governor John A. Andrew and other New England abolitionists and free blacks.

After the War Department authorized the Massachusetts governor to raise black regiments, the efforts to raise the first such regiment were centered in Boston. Frederick Douglass was one of the regiment's recruiters. He scoured the North on a sacred mission, seeking free black men who would fight the Rebels and strike a blow against slavery. Douglass wrote a famous appeal that appeared in newspapers across the North, exhorting "Men of Color, to Arms!"

Recruitment efforts were made across the North and even in Canada, which many African Americans had reached by way of the Underground Railroad. To prove the worth of

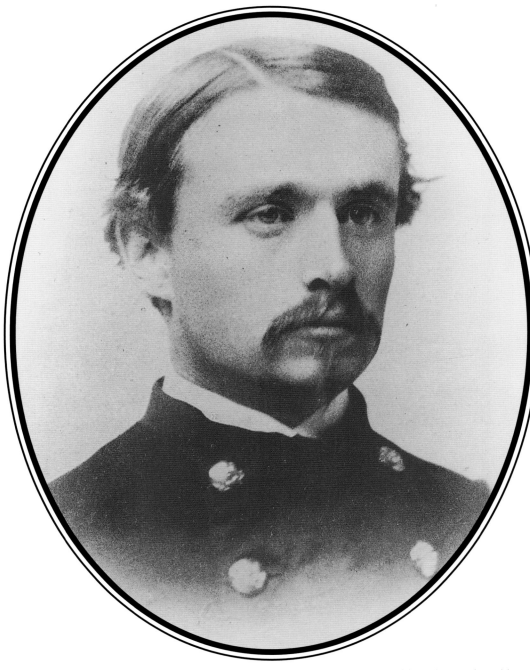

PAGE 53: Leading by example, Colonel Robert Gould Shaw encouraged his soldiers forward until he was felled at the head of his troops during the fierce charge of the 54th Massachusetts at Fort Wagner. ABOVE: The young Colonel Robert Gould Shaw left behind privilege, wealth, and his influential abolitionist parents in fashionable Boston to lead the 54th Massachusetts. Shaw molded the regiment into the kind of highly trained and motivated fighting force that convinced the Northern politicians to mass-enlist black troops.

the African American fighting man, Governor Andrew was determined to secure the best recruits possible, making the 54th Massachusetts a model regiment for the scores of African American units that would soon be formed throughout the Union.

Recruitment was initially slow, however. It was 1863, the midpoint of the war, and for both blacks and whites, enthusiasm for the conflict had waned. A number of other factors, which did not apply to white soldiers, helped curtail recruitment among African Americans. For instance, the Confederate Congress voted in May 1863 that captured blacks would be killed, or even enslaved, by the Confederacy. Captured white officers of black regiments were to be "put to death or be otherwise punished" by Confederate authorities. This vengeful policy stemmed from the South's fear that black Yankee invaders would spark slave revolt across the South.

Since free blacks in the North already enjoyed a large degree of freedom, they were not eager to serve in a black Massachusetts regiment destined to march into the Deep South, where slavery had thrived. They were also hesitant to join because they realized that enlistment meant forfeiting some of their rights as citizen: to a free black man in the North, military service under white officers seemed somewhat akin to slavery.

Nevertheless, African Americans joined the 54th Massachusetts. With determination and pride, volunteers like James Henry Hall enlisted. Hall explained that he joined the regiment to win and ensure "the proper enjoyment of the rights of citizenship, and a free title and acknowledged share in our own noble birthplace."

Additional African American recruits came forward from Philadelphia, New York City, Buffalo, Detroit, Cincinnati, and St. Louis. All these men volunteered despite rumors that they might be killed, imprisoned, or even enslaved if captured by the Rebels. The volunteers in the 54th Massachusetts were free blacks, and only a handful of them had experienced the horrors of slavery or even seen the Deep South. These free Northern blacks had been artisans, farmers, blacksmiths, teamsters, boatmen and whaling men, laborers, barbers, butchers, and cooks.

The African Americans who joined the 54th Massachusetts were idealistic and highly motivated. They believed that this was an opportunity to strike the blow that could end the hated institution of slavery forever. A black journalist from the *Anglo-African* appealed to the revolutionary tradition of black heroism in America's past wars, writing,

> *Should we not with two centuries of cruel wrong stirring our heart's blood, be but too willing to embrace any chance to settle accounts with the slaveholders?…Why should we be alarmed at their threat of hanging us; do we intend to become their prisoners? Such is not the record our black fathers made in the revolutionary war nor is such the record of those who fought under [Andrew] Jackson in the War of 1812….*

Two of the new recruits of the 54th Massachusetts were the sons of Frederick Douglass. Charles and Lewis Douglass, who were among the first volunteers from New York, now served as sergeants in the ranks of the 54th. Like the other soldiers of the 54th Massachusetts, the sons of Douglass would risk their lives on the battlefield fighting, in the words of Lewis, "for God, liberty, and country…."

The poet James Henry Gooding, age twenty-six, was another determined free black man of the 54th Massachusetts. Originally from Troy, New York, he had

come to New Bedford, Massachusetts, in 1856 to work as a whaler. On whaling voyages around the world, he wrote poetry about the sea and a sailor's life. He enlisted in Company C, 54th Massachusetts, for the honor of "carrying a musket in defense of liberty and right"; he served as a corporal. Company C consisted of many New Bedford soldiers of the "Toussaint Guards," named for the "Black Napoleon," Toussaint L'Ouverture, who had defeated the French and liberated the slaves of St. Domingue, to establish Haiti, the first black republic.

In a revealing letter published in the *New Bedford Mercury* of March 15, 1863, from the regiment's training camp at Readville, Massachusetts, Corporal Gooding explained how the men of the 54th were "all anxious to perfect themselves in drill that they may the sooner meet the Rebs, and they all feel determined to fight…they have an impulse equally as great [which] is revenge."

Gooding wrote that this war would see "but two results possible, one is slavery and poverty and the other is liberty and prosperity." He survived the great attack on Fort Wagner but not the war. After his capture at the Battle of Olustee, Florida, in February 1864, Gooding was destined to die amid the squalor and horror of Andersonville Prison, deep in Georgia, during the summer of 1864.

LEFT TOP: Lieutenant Colonel Norwood Penrose Hallowell, who was Colonel Shaw's top lieutenant during the attack on Fort Wagner. He was born in Philadelphia, Pennsylvania, in 1839 and served in the 20th Massachusetts Volunteer Infantry and as colonel of the 55th Massachusetts Volunteer Infantry. Hallowell was discharged after he was wounded during the Battle of Antietam; he then joined Colonel Shaw's regiment. LEFT BOTTOM: Massachusetts-born Captain Luis F. Emilio, the son of a Spanish immigrant, served with distinction as the commander of Company E, 54th Massachusetts Volunteer Infantry. He was one of the survivors of the attack on Fort Wagner.

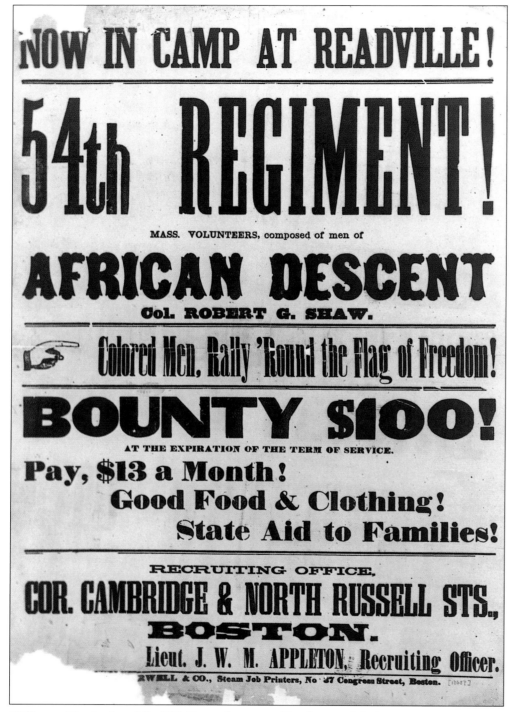

The 1863 recruiting poster of the 54th Massachusetts, calling for men "of African Descent" and "Colored Men [to] Rally Round the Flag of Freedom!" A bounty of $100.00 was offered, along with the attractive lure of a salary, food, clothing, and aid for soldiers' families.

Robert Gould Shaw was chosen by Governor Andrew to be the colonel and first commander of the 54th Massachusetts. The recently married Shaw was the privileged son of wealthy abolitionist parents from Boston. Educated at Harvard and in Europe, and possessing refinement, taste, and a noble bearing, Shaw was a Boston blueblood. He had had little experience working with African Americans, and even his military experience was limited: he had served only as a captain in the 2nd Massachusetts. Nevertheless, young Colonel Shaw proved an excellent choice to mold the 54th Massachusetts into the regiment that would win glory at Fort Wagner.

On May 28, 1863, with firm discipline and precision, the 54th Massachusetts marched through Boston on the way to the seat of war. Accompanied by the inspiring strains of "John Brown's Body" and the wild cheers of a large crowd, the men of the 54th Massachusetts presented a fine appearance. Hundreds of black soldiers marched through the streets of Boston with new Enfield rifles on their shoulders, under a flag embroidered with the words, "Liberty, Loyalty, and Unity."

Thousands of black and white Northerners cheered as the first black regiment from the North marched to the wharf to board steamboats for the long journey to Hilton Head, South Carolina. Among the crowd was the author of *Incidents in the Life of a Slave Girl*, Harriet Jacobs. She wrote emotionally, "How my heart swelled with the thought that my poor oppressed race were to strike a blow for Freedom!"

According to Captain Luis Fenollosa Emilio of Company E, during the memorable march through Boston, the African Americans in blue passed "over ground moistened by the blood of Crispus Attucks," who had fallen here eighty-eight years before. Frederick Douglass looked on with pride not only at the fulfillment of his long-sought dream, but also because his two sons marched in the ranks. Nearby, the great abolitionist William Lloyd Garrison watched from the balcony of his home while resting his hand on a bust of John Brown. Prophetically, in a May 24, 1863, letter, Corporal Gooding wrote:

It seems that most every man in the regiment vies with each other in excellence in whatever they undertake [therefore] I feel confident the Colored Volunteers will add glory to [the regiment's] already bright name [even] if captured by the foe, and they will die upon the field rather than be hanged like a dog; and when a thousand men are fighting for a very existence [then] the greatest difficulty will be to stop them.

After their arrival in sweltering South Carolina, the 54th Massachusetts served beside their fellow African American soldiers from South Carolina under Colonel James Montgomery. He had waged a vicious guerrilla war on the Missouri-Kansas border and was now doing the same in South Carolina with his black regiment. The idealistic Colonel Shaw felt considerable frustration as the 54th Massachusetts was forced to engage in such ruthless activities as the burning of Darien, Georgia, even though these actions were sanctioned by General David Hunter, who was the department commander. Shaw longed to enhance the status of his regiment and wipe away the stain of the burning of Darien. That eagerly sought opportunity came with the great challenge at Fort Wagner.

In July 1863, the Union's objective was to capture the key city of Charleston, South Carolina. But first, Morris Island, which lay south of Charleston Harbor and guarded its entrance, had to be captured. Union leaders expected relatively light resistance on Morris Island, and once the island was seized, a

Drummer boys like this determined young man marched in the front ranks of the 54th Massachusetts before the regiment launched its bloody assault on Fort Wagner.

massive array of Federal batteries could be set up there to pound Fort Sumter into submission from the south. After Fort Sumter fell and the forces of Confederate General Pierre G.T. Beauregard were defeated, then Charleston could easily be captured by the Union navy.

On July 16, 1863, the 54th Massachusetts received its baptism of fire. The rookie regiment fought with distinction on James Island, northwest of Morris Island. One white soldier declared that the men of the 54th "fought like heroes," saving his Connecticut regiment during a fierce Rebel attack.

After the hot fight on James Island, Sergeant Simmons of Company B, 54th Massachusetts, wrote to his mother that "God has protected me through this, my first fiery, leaden trial, and I do give Him the glory." A white captain called Sergeant Simmons the "finest-looking soldier in the Fifty-fourth,—a brave man and of good education." Simmons would later be cited for gallantry at Fort Wagner, but he would also be captured. He would die in a dingy Charleston prison in August 1863, after having an arm amputated.

After winning at James Island, the Union captured Folly Island, and finally the Federals were in position to move north to Morris Island. Both of these barrier islands—Folly to the south and Morris to the north—were stepping stones to the reduction of Fort Wagner. Wagner had to be taken. A powerful bastion on the Atlantic coast, it guarded the other Rebel forts that protected Charleston Harbor. If Fort Wagner was captured, Fort Sumter could be reduced, and then Charleston would fall. This was a good plan, and the 54th Massachusetts would play a key role in attempting to make this ambitious scheme a reality during that hot July in steamy South Carolina.

Fort Wagner stood defiantly on the north end of Morris Island. On the day of destiny, July 18, the 54th Massachusetts was transported by steamboat to the southern end of Morris Island. Replacing General Hunter, Major General Quincy Adams Gillmore was assigned to lead the land forces of the Department of the South in the attempt to capture Charleston.

The 54th Massachusetts quickly assembled on the sun-baked sands of Morris Island, then marched northward along the beach to the headquarters of Brigade Commander General George Crockett Strong, who had been chosen to lead the attack on Fort Wagner. In a July 20 letter to the *New Bedford Mercury*, Corporal Gooding wrote:

On Saturday afternoon we were marched up past our batteries, amid the cheers of the officers and soldiers. We wondered what they were all cheering for, but we soon found out. Gen. Strong rode up, and we halted [and he then] asked us if we would follow him into Fort Wagner. Every man said, yes—we were ready to follow wherever we were led.

Recent attacks by General Strong's regiments had been unsuccessful, ending in bloody repulses. Nevertheless, Colonel Shaw remained eager for this challenge. He believed that his Massachusetts regiment could do what the more seasoned white troops had been unable to do: capture Fort Wagner by storm. Shaw ignored the fact that his men had had little rest during the last three days and no food in the last twenty-four hours. Young Shaw was eager to lead the attack himself, although he was haunted by a dark premonition that he would not survive the assault.

A promising officer and former West Pointer, Strong was impressed by the fighting spirit and combat capability that the 54th Massachusetts had recently demonstrated on James Island. Saying the words that Shaw longed to hear, General Strong told the young colonel, "You may lead the [attack] column if you say 'yes.' Your men, I know are worn out; but do as you choose." Colonel Shaw said "yes," welcoming the opportunity to prove the worth and combat prowess of the 54th Massachusetts, not only to the North and South, but also to the world.

Governor Andrew had risked his political career on the single hope that the 54th Massachusetts would rise to this challenge. Writing to Colonel Shaw, Andrew stated, "I know not, Mr. Commander, where in all human history, to any given thousand men in arms there has been committed a work at

MORRIS ISLAND
Relative positions of the Union and Confederate forces surrounding Fort Wagner, July 1863

Approximate scale in miles

0   ½

■■ **Union**   ▬▬ **Confederate**

This map of Fort Wagner, on Morris Island, shows how thoroughly the terrain and topography favored the defenders and hampered the attack of the 54th Massachusetts.

A concentration of Federal artillery, such as this cannon on Morris Island, was to have reduced Fort Wagner as planned by Union leadership to allow the 54th Massachusetts to easily capture the bastion. Unfortunately, however, this was not the case.

once so proud, so precious, so full of hope and glory as the work committed to you." And in the words of Captain Emilio, "The whole question of employing three hundred thousand colored soldiers hung in the balance." Indeed, perhaps even the fate of the Union "hung in the balance."

A reporter for the *New York Herald* placed the significance of the upcoming battle in a proper historical perspective:

There were regiments from [Massachusetts] which had seen more fighting than this, though none which had done any better fighting when occasion offered; none which had a higher reputation for discipline, patient endurance, and impetuous valor. But the true reason why Massachusetts singled out this regiment for peculiar honor is because this was the first colored regiment organized in the North, and was that one on whose good conduct depended for a long time the success of the whole experiment of arming black citizens in defense of the Republic [and] it made Fort Wagner such a name to the colored race as Bunker Hill has been for ninety years to the white Yankees,—albeit black men fought side by side with white in the trenches on that 17th of June.

At this time, the North was still largely racist, discriminatory, and hostile to black people. The wives and children of black Union soldiers were not spared the poorhouse while their husbands, brothers, and fathers risked their lives for the nation. During the New York draft riots, white rioters destroyed black people's homes, and some African Americans were attacked and lynched by white mobs. Nevertheless, the optimistic soldiers of the 54th Massachusetts believed that at Fort Wagner they now had both the opportunity and the power to change things for the better for themselves and oppressed blacks throughout the North and South. In the words of Governor Andrews: "Its success

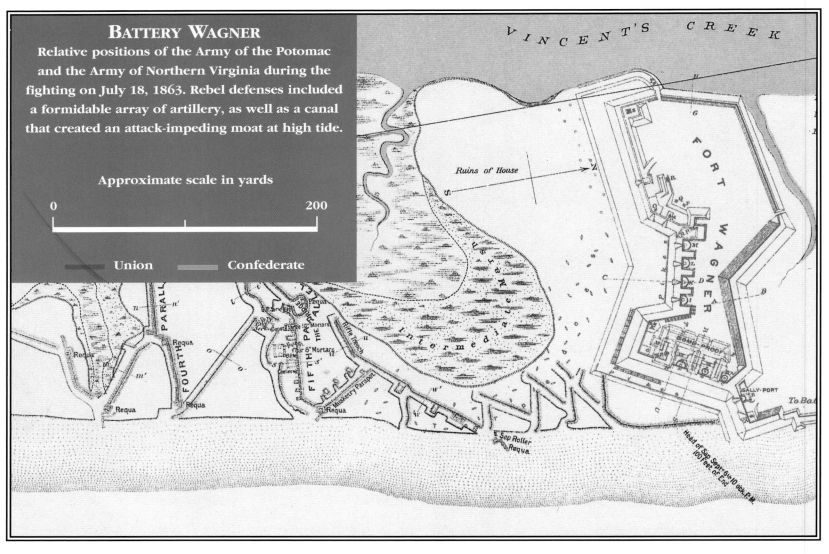

BATTERY WAGNER

Relative positions of the Army of the Potomac and the Army of Northern Virginia during the fighting on July 18, 1863. Rebel defenses included a formidable array of artillery, as well as a canal that created an attack-impeding moat at high tide.

Approximate scale in yards

0   200

▬▬ Union   ▬▬ Confederate

or its failure will go far to elevate or depress the estimation in which the character of the colored Americans will be held throughout the world."

On July 2, 1863, in a letter to the governor, Colonel Shaw related that General Strong was "anxious to do all he can for us, and if there is a fight in the Department will no doubt give the black troops a chance to show what stuff they are made of." Indeed, Fort Wagner was now the ideal arena for the men of the 54th Massachusetts to fully

demonstrate before the eyes of the nation and the world exactly "what stuff they are made of."

Embarking on this formidable challenge, the soldiers of the 54th Massachusetts marched bravely forward on Fort Wagner with flags flying. The men of the lone Massachusetts regiment moved onward with a disciplined step, just as they had marched through Boston barely fifty days before. These African Americans were on their way to prove to the nation that they were the

equals of white soldiers. With noble bearing, they marched past the white units that were to support them in the great assault, trudging onward in silence and firm resolution. At a distance of six hundred yards (540m) south of the imposing Confederate bastion, Colonel Shaw halted his regiment.

Also known as Battery Wagner, Fort Wagner was the most powerful fortification on Morris Island. The defending sixteen-hundred-man force consisted of Georgia, South Carolina, and North Carolina

OPPOSITE: Detailed map of Fort Wagner, indicating the bastion's imposing strength and powerful configuration. The narrowness of the beach constricted the assault formations of the 54th Massachusetts, making compact targets for Confederate artillery and small arms. ABOVE: Photograph of the entrance of the massive main bombproof redoubt at Fort Wagner, which afforded safety for the Rebel garrison. Such a shelter thwarted the effectiveness of the intense Federal bombardment that was to have weakened the garrison and bastion, while opening the way for the attack of the 54th Massachusetts. In this photograph, a group of black soldiers of the 54th Massachusetts stands to the left.

infantrymen and artillerymen under the recently arrived General William B. Taliaferro. He was a Virginian and one of Stonewall Jackson's old lieutenants from the Shenandoah Valley campaign of 1862.

Named in honor of Charleston native Lieutenant Colonel Thomas M. Wagner, 1st South Carolina Artillery, who had been mortally wounded in July 1862, Fort Wagner was well constructed. The fort was bolstered by sandbags and palmetto logs, which could easily absorb the heaviest pounding from large-caliber guns and the Union navy's cannon. The large-caliber guns of Fort Wagner faced east toward the Atlantic, and the land approach was covered by a formidable array of mobile howitzers and field pieces. Large-caliber and naval guns in fixed positions also faced south, enabling defenders to sweep enemy forces making the approach up the beach. In addition, a canal was cut before the fort, creating a moat of seawater at high tide to further impede any attacks. At the northern end of Morris Island, Battery Gregg protected Fort Wagner's rear. Well-placed shelters protected the garrison from the punishment of artillery from both land batteries and the Union navy's ironclads, which were aligned off the Atlantic coast.

Positioned just below Battery Gregg and Cumming's Point at the island's northern edge, Battery Wagner stood on the Atlantic Coast, only about one mile (1.6km) from and

LEFT: Sergeant Henry Steward, Company E, 54th Massachusetts. He was a twenty-three-year-old farmer and bachelor from Adrian, Michigan. Sergeant Steward died of disease on February 18, 1865, in a hospital on Morris Island, South Carolina. ABOVE: Sergeant William Henry Carney, Company C, 54th Massachusetts. This twenty-two-year-old seaman from New Bedford—a former Virginia slave—was one of the heroes of Fort Wagner, winning the Congressional Medal of Honor for valor. He was wounded during the attack but survived to save the regimental colors at great risk to his life.

almost directly south of Fort Sumter and Charleston Harbor. The slender width of the sandy, windswept barrier island enhanced the defensive strength of Fort Wagner. The line of powerful Rebel defenses that was Wagner spanned the entire width of the narrow barrier island. The ocean on the east protected the fort's left flank while a saltwater marsh protected its right. Consequently, attackers who advanced north toward the southern end of Fort Wagner would be funneled toward the fort and its bristling rows of artillery.

Fort Wagner had to be captured to ensure the fall of Charleston, since the fort dominated the sea approaches to the city. Charleston was a key Atlantic port for block-ade runners laden with supplies, weaponry, and materiel from Europe. Charleston was also the political and philosophical birthplace of secession, and the Civil War began there when Confederate guns unleashed their wrath on Fort Sumter in mid-April 1861. That first Union loss of the war had to be avenged; this nest of treason had to be stamped out.

But the defenders of Fort Wagner were also thinking about vengeance. The Rebels were determined to hold out at all costs. With the sun dropping in the west and the light of the hot July day fading away, the men of the 54th Massachusetts prepared for action, forming into two lines of battle. Bayonets were fixed, and the clanging as these deadly implements were placed on the barrels of six hundred Enfield rifles rang across Morris Island.

Fate was not kind to the black regiment. The force was too weak for success, and the Union leadership's overall plan for the assault was ill-conceived. The column was of insuffi-cient strength because Union diversions had been made to disguise the exact point of the attack on Morris Island and to draw defenders away. The narrow beach offered the only avenue for the attackers to strike Fort Wagner from the south, and it was a natural killing field. Captain Emilio, a bachelor stu-dent from Salem, Massachusetts, described the narrow front and the sandy beach, which "at low tide…afforded a good pathway to the enemy's position [but] at high tide, it was through deep, loose sand, and over low sand hillocks." The 54th Massachusetts would storm forward at high tide.

Undeterred by the earlier bloody repulse of a similarly doomed frontal assault, General Gillmore was determined that Fort Wagner would be taken at all costs, and decided to try the same plan of attack. He handed General Truman Seymour the job of organiz-ing the details for the assaulting column. And Seymour, who was impressed by General Strong's role in earlier attacks on Fort Wagner, had handed the West Pointer the job of taking Fort Wagner.

For the renewed attack on Fort Wagner, Gillmore and Seymour sent the regiments of Strong's brigade, which consisted of troops from Massachusetts, New York, Maine, Pennsylvania, New Hampshire, and Connecticut. It was to be one of the war's most difficult missions. Like many other Civil War generals, Gillmore remained uncon-vinced of a new tactical reality: with the advances in weaponry, direct frontal assaults across open ground by infantry against a strong defensive position were suicidal.

In a futile attempt to knock out the guns and defenders of Fort Wagner, Union artillery and ironclads pounded Fort Wagner with nearly one thousand shells of all sizes throughout the day. Though little damage was done, the overly optimistic General Gillmore expected scant resistance from

Fort Wagner and believed that the next infantry assault would be successful. But Fort Wagner stood almost as formidable as before the daylong artillery bombardment.

General Strong was to lead the first assault wave of seven regiments during the evening attack on Fort Wagner. A second assault wave was also readied for action. At the front of the first attack column, with fixed bayonets, the men of the 54th Massachusetts grimly awaited the signal to lead the attack on the most powerful fortress that they had ever seen. Colonel Shaw chal-lenged his men to "take the fort or die there." The soldiers of the 54th felt consider-able responsibility, but also a great deal of pride. Captain Emilio wrote that his regiment "had been given the post of honor" in the upcoming attack on Fort Wagner.

Destined to be fatally wounded in the attack, General Strong, who was himself from Massachusetts, rode up to the two assault formations of the 54th. After giving final instructions to Colonel Shaw, Strong turned to the men of the regiment, inspiring them with his conviction that they would uphold the honor of their home state in the upcom-ing charge. The general said, "Don't fire a musket on the way up, but go in and bayo-net them at their guns." Consequently, the

Sketch of the Federal artillery bombardment that rained a barrage of shells upon Fort Wagner before the attack, giving Union leadership false confidence for the assault.

577 Enfield rifles of the African Americans in blue were not loaded.

General Strong then pointed to a black color sergeant, John Wall, a twenty-year-old student from Oberlin, Ohio, and yelled to the soldiers of the 54th Massachusetts, "If this man should fall, who will lift the flag and carry it on?" Immediately accepting the challenge, Colonel Shaw answered, "I will!" With his spirited response, the African American soldiers cheered their young commander, whom they now respected more than ever.

Colonel Shaw went over to his second in command, Lieutenant Colonel Edward N. Hallowell, and said, "I shall go in advance with the National flag. You will keep the State flag with you....We shall take the fort or die there! Good-bye!"

Then Shaw, resplendent in his new blue colonel's uniform, looked over the attack formations of his determined soldiers. He told his men, "I want you to prove yourself. The eyes of thousands will be on what you do tonight." Ignoring a premonition of death, the colonel stood before his men in the eerie half-darkness, with only the sound of splashing waves breaking the haunting stillness. The Union guns had ceased firing and the ironclads began to disengage and pull out to sea. Colonel Shaw was about to lead what had seldom succeeded in this war, a direct bayonet attack against a powerful fortified position.

Captain Emilio recalled feeling uneasy about the lack of preparations for the attack because "there was no provision for cutting away obstructions, filling the ditch, or spiking the guns." But Union leaders continued to believe that Fort Wagner could be easily overwhelmed by a direct frontal attack, and

Sketches of the fortifications of Fort Wagner, showing detailed views of artillery emplacements, bombproof shelters, moat, abatis obstacles, and the size and strength of the bastion.

the second assault was about to be launched against the odds and with almost no hope for success.

With drums and bugles sounding the call, hundreds of Rebels poured out of their shelters to take firing positions to defend Fort Wagner. Cheering and ready for the fight, the Confederates, eager for revenge on the Yankees who had been punishing them for most of the day, rushed to their firing positions to meet the attack.

Captain Emilio later remembered the surreal setting at twilight, as the 54th Massachusetts prepared to undertake its greatest challenge:

Away over the sea to the eastward the heavy sea-fog was gathering, the western sky bright with the reflected light, for the sun had set...all was ominous of the impending onslaught. Far and indistinct in front was the now silent earthwork, seamed, scarred, and ploughed with shot, its flag still waving in defiance.

The night shrouded the beach in blackness. It was 7:45 p.m. when a determined

Colonel Shaw finally drew his saber. He shouted for all to hear, "Move in quick-time until within a hundred yards [90m] of the fort; then double-quick and charge!" With this fateful order, the nearly six hundred soldiers of the 54th Massachusetts attacked with bayonets fixed to their rifles and the resolve to do or die. Shaw, remaining in front, led the lead battalion of five companies forward with a shout. Meanwhile, Lieutenant Colonel Hallowell led the second battalion of five companies forward, following the lead battalion.

The attack column of the 54th Massachusetts surged forward. Almost immediately, it was revealed how little Fort Wagner had been damaged by the Union bombardment. Rebel cannon bellowed defiance from the sand and log parapets, pouring forth a deadly rain of shells. On the double-quick, the African Americans in blue surged onward through the exploding shells, with state and national flags flowing proudly above them. All the while, the roar of Confederate cannon grew louder.

As the Union soldiers neared the blazing fortification, the ranks were squeezed tightly together between the salt marsh and the sea. This constriction provided more compact

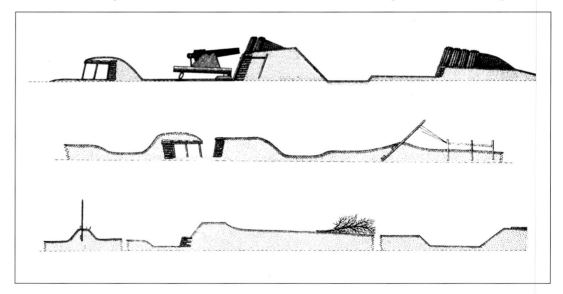

targets for Confederate marksmen. On the regiment's right, attacking soldiers staggered forward though knee-deep water, racing through the surf, which was pounding both the beach and the salt marsh. These natural obstacles seriously impeded the advance, and all the while Rebel shells continued to explode amid the surging ranks, blowing holes in formations and knocking down soldiers in every direction.

Nevertheless, Colonel Shaw and his men continued onward in the darkness, rushing through the exploding shells that caused so much destruction. In a letter written to his future wife, Amelia, shortly after the battle, Sergeant Major Lewis Douglass—one of the sons of Frederick Douglass—described his horror as hundreds of Rebel defenders let loose a "perfect hail of shot and shell."

It was terrible [but] not a man flinched, though it was a trying time. Men fell all around me. A shell would explode and clear a space of twenty feet [6m], our men would close up again.... The ramparts of Wagner flashed with [fire] and all the large shotted guns roared with defiance. Sumter and Cumming's Point delivered a destructive cross-fire, while the howitzers in the bastions raked [the assaulting formations.]

As if this were not enough punishment, African American soldiers were also falling from the fire of their own artillery. An angry Corporal Gooding recorded in a letter that the column was "exposed to a murderous fire from the batteries of the fort [and] from

The 54th Massachusetts assaults Fort Wagner, with attackers crossing the moat before swarming up the parapet. Near the top of the fiery parapet, Colonel Shaw, with uplifted saber, falls before his men.

Private William J. Nelson, a member of a regimental band of the 54th Massachusetts. As a regimental musician, he was spared the nightmare of the costly frontal assault on Fort Wagner.

our Monitors and our land batteries, as they did not cease firing soon enough."

But the worst was yet to come. As the exposed 54th Massachusetts approached the works, Fort Wagner's commander, General Taliaferro, at last ordered the defenders aligned along the parapet to open fire. Illuminating the night in surreal horror, the first great eruption of musketry from Fort Wagner exploded like thunder, dropping dozens of attacking soldiers to the ground and lighting up the parapet for hundreds of feet.

Captain Emilio watched in horror as his men of Company E were cut down. He never forgot how "a sheet of flame, followed by a running fire, like electric sparks, swept along the parapet." Nevertheless, through the din, carnage, and fallen bodies, the black soldiers continued their double-quick charge toward fire-streaked Fort Wagner. Indeed, now "the swifter pace was taken, and officers sprung to the fore with waving swords barely seen in the darkness, the men closed the gaps, and with set jaws, panting breath, and bowed heads, charged on."

Inspiring regimental leaders such as Lieutenant Colonel Hallowell and Color Sergeant Wall fell to the ground covered in blood. This severe punishment was too much for these men caught out in the open, with no protection, to endure. The determined assault of the 54th Massachusetts stalled and sputtered, while the bodies piled up around the hard-hit survivors.

All the while, a storm of musketry, canister, and shell shot continued to drop more bluecoats in what was fast becoming a slaughter. One soldier described the nightmare, as hundreds of Rebels of Fort Wagner simply "mowed us down like grass." Corporal Gooding later wrote that "at the first charge the 54th rushed to within twenty yards [6m] of the ditches, and as might be expected of raw recruits, wavered" under the deadly fire streaming from the fortifications.

Photograph of the interior of Fort Wagner, which the attackers of the 54th Massachusetts penetrated despite the fall of Colonel Shaw, heavy casualties, and unfavorable odds.

Captain James William Grace, a thirty-three-year-old merchant from New Bedford, described how the attackers surged forward "with a tremendous scream [and] when we arrived within a short distance of the works, the Rebels opened on us with grape and canister accompanied with a thousand muskets, mowing our men down by the hundreds. This caused us to fall back a little...."

Rising to the challenge, Colonel Shaw took the initiative. He knew that something had to be done, and soon—the exposed regiment must either immediately retreat in failure or advance onward to win glory. Leading by example, swinging his saber, and shouting encouragement, Shaw led his men forward once again, resuming the attack amid the hail of lead.

Raising a cheer, the black soldiers followed their fearless colonel, surging through the water-filled moat before Fort Wagner. All the while, hundreds of Confederates continued to unleash a terrible fire against the exposed attackers. More soldiers fell wounded, including Sergeant Major Lewis Douglass, the son of the famous black revolutionary and abolitionist. Blue-clad bodies began to

fill the moat; they floated in the blood-stained water and impeded the advance of the determined band of survivors.

Shouting, "Onward boys!" Colonel Shaw led his attackers up the parapet. Here, a vicious flurry of hand-to-hand fighting erupted when blue and gray clashed in the nightmarish darkness and hell that was Fort Wagner. Blacks jabbed with bayonets, and Confederates brained Yankees with musket butts during the savage melee. Colonel Shaw stood tall near the top of the parapet encouraging his soldiers onward and up the bullet-swept slope of Fort Wagner and waving his sword for all to see.

Corporal Gooding described the dramatic turning point of the bloody struggle in a July 1863 letter to the *New Bedford Mercury*. He wrote, "At the second advance [we] gained the parapet. Col. Shaw seized the staff when the standard bearer fell, and in less than a minute after, the Colonel fell himself." Captain Emilio wrote that upon "gaining the parapet, [Colonel Shaw] stood there for a moment with uplifted sword, shouting 'Forward, Fifty-fourth!' and then fell dead, shot through the heart, besides other wounds." Colonel Shaw suffered as many as seven wounds, falling to rise no more.

Shaw had led the attack into the vortex of the storm, encouraging his men to strike the fiery center of Fort Wagner. At age twenty-six, Colonel Shaw was cut down, but his inspiration remained. His black soldiers continued up the slope with fixed bayonets and the staunch determination to capture Fort Wagner at all costs.

The loss of their leader only stirred the desire for revenge among the survivors as they fought in vain to retrieve the young colonel's body. As Corporal Gooding wrote

"The color bearer of the State colors was killed on the parapet. Col. Shaw seized the staff when the standard bearer fell, and in less than a minute after, the Colonel fell himself. When the men saw their gallant leader fall, they made a desperate effort to get him out, but they were either shot down, or reeled in the ditch below."

—Corporal James Henry Gooding

In this dramatic painting by Tom Lovell , Colonel Robert Gould Shaw leads his soldiers of the 54th Massachusetts over the blazing parapet of Fort Wagner, where hand-to-hand combat raged fiercely.

in that letter of July 1863, "When the men saw their gallant leader fall, they made a desperate effort to get him out, but they were either shot down, or reeled in the ditch below. One man succeeded in getting hold of the State color staff, but the color was completely torn to pieces."

Resolute natural leaders like Virginia-born Sergeant William Henry Carney of Company C, a twenty-two-year-old seaman from New Bedford, now filled the void. After the fall of Color Sergeant Wall, Carney had picked up the flag to inspire his comrades forward into the raging storm. One of the first to join the regiment and, unlike most of his free black comrades, a former Virginia slave, he took the colors all the way to the flaming parapet. Despite four wounds, Sergeant Carney protected the colors of the 54th Massachusetts with his life, earning the Congressional Medal of Honor for his heroism.

The fierce attack of the 54th Massachusetts continued rolling forward. One black sergeant, George E. Stephens of Company B, remembered the brutal fighting inside Fort Wagner: "Many of the men [had] clambered over [the parapet] and some entered by the large embrasure in which one of the big guns was mounted [when] an officer of our regiment called out, 'Spike that gun!'" More close-quarter combat followed in the surreal darkness. Captain Emilio recalled that "musket-butts and bayonets were freely used on the parapet [as] the garrison fought with muskets, handspikes, and gun-rammers, the officers striking with their swords...." Dependable leaders such as Captain Cabot Jackson Russel, a former student from Boston leading Company H, and Captain William Harris Simpkins, an ex-clerk from Boston leading Company K, were killed amid the slaughter, falling near their beloved Colonel Shaw on the body-strewn slope of Fort Wagner.

Despite the heroism and glory, the attack was repulsed. The 54th Massachusetts had suffered heavy losses. The assault had been launched with too few attackers and was poorly planned by Union leadership. It began with an ineffective bombardment and

Union troops in formation at Fort Wagner. A key objective of Colonel Shaw and the 54th Massachusetts was the capture of the interior of Fort Wagner, which would have ensured the fall of the powerful bastion.

ended without timely infantry support to exploit the initial gains won by the attack column. This combination of Union tactical errors and miscalculations allowed the Confederates to counterattack. In hand-to-hand fighting that raged across the sandy walls of Fort Wagner on that desperate night, the Union forces were hurled back.

With so many men cut down, Captain Emilio, the ninth captain in terms of seniority, assumed regimental command. He now realized that "numbers, however, soon told against the Fifty-fourth, for it was tens against hundreds [as] the garrison was stronger than had been supposed, and brave in defending the work."

Like the first assault wave of Federals, the second was repulsed, increasing the casualty lists for no gain. Of the 5,000 attackers on that bloody day, more than fifteen hundred Yankees were killed or wounded. The 54th Massachusetts suffered severely during the doomed assault. In winning glory

and everlasting fame, the 54th Massachusetts lost a staggering 42 percent of its enlisted strength and fourteen of twenty-two officers. Of the almost 600 attackers of the 54th Massachusetts, 272 soldiers were killed, wounded, or captured during the suicidal assault. In the words of Captain Emilio, the struggle for Fort Wagner was "one of the fiercest struggles of the war, considering the numbers engaged."

In the end, though, many people—and not only Northerners—were impressed by the valor of the 54th Massachusetts. Even Confederates bestowed a measure of recognition and respect upon the black soldiers. One Rebel officer wrote that "the negroes fought gallantly and were headed by as brave a colonel as ever lived. He mounted the breastworks waving his sword, and at the head of his regiment, and he and a negro orderly sergeant fell dead over the inner crest of the works."

For the soldiers of the 54th Massachusetts, the tragic loss of Colonel Shaw was more painful even than the high casualties. Only later was it confirmed that he was dead and not captured. An infuriated Corporal Gooding wrote in a July 24 letter, "We have learned by the flag-of-truce boat that Colonel Shaw is dead—he was buried in a trench with 45 of his men! Not even the commonest respect paid to his rank [and] the men of the regiment [now] declare that they will dig for his body till they find it." Colonel Shaw had been buried with the men that he loved and led to glory at an obscure place now washed away by the sea.

However, the 54th Massachusetts won much more than glory at Fort Wagner. The men of the regiment had truly demonstrated the resolve, combat capabilities, and fighting prowess of the Union's African American soldiers. More than ever before, the North was convinced of the merit of enlisting large numbers of black troops, and the 54th

Massachusetts would now be memorialized, respected, and idealized across the North.

The war-weary North had suddenly gained new heroes in a war effort that had grown old and tiresome. The North also embraced the new moral ideology of equality, which was essential to winning the war. Captain Emilio of Company E had been correct. What was at stake at Fort Wagner had been nothing short of the "whole question of employing three hundred thousand colored soldiers."

Colonel Shaw's death and the gallantry of the 54th Massachusetts at Fort Wagner on July 18, 1863, opened the floodgates for the enlistment of tens of thousands of African Americans who would ensure that the North would win the Civil War.

And these African Americans would not be designated for secondary roles. They participated in the great battles that remained in the last two years of the war.

Indeed, after Fort Wagner, black troops won distinction on the battlefields of Olustee, Florida; Brice's Cross Roads, Mississippi; Nashville, Tennessee; Petersburg, Virginia; Spanish Fort and Fort Blakeley, Alabama; and in hundreds of other battles and skirmishes across the South. A black regiment, the 62nd United States Colored Infantry, fought in the last battle of the Civil War, at Palmito Ranch, Texas, on May 13, 1865, firing the last volley of the war.

For their efforts during the war, two dozen African Americans were awarded the Congressional Medal of Honor, winning glory for themselves and for their nation. Glory came at a high price, however: 70,000 men, more than one-third of all black troops in U.S. service, became casualties. But without the contributions and sacrifices of the more than 200,000 African American soldiers who risked their lives for the Union and for freedom, the North would not have won the Civil War.

chapter 4

BLACK CONFEDERATES

One of the forgotten stories of the Civil War is the story of black Confederates. While the Union is more often credited with the enlistment and use of black troops, the contributions that African Americans made to the Confederacy's war effort were also significant. In the words of one Northern black, "The institution of slavery in the South alone enables her to place in the field a force much larger in proportion to her white population than the North [can place, and] the institution is a tower of strength to the South." Without the support of Southern blacks, both free and slave, the Confederacy could not have waged its war of attrition for four long years.

Four million African Americans all across the South—from the Atlantic coast to the Rio Grande in Texas—supported the Confederate war machine and the fledgling nation during its life-and-death struggle. Their labors in the fields, railroad yards, factories, wharves, sweatshops, arsenals, and hospitals of the South fueled the rebel war effort.

But what has generally been overlooked in the Civil War historiography is the fact that thousands of African Americans served faithfully and with distinction in the armies and navies of the Confederacy. From the moment the first shots were fired on Fort Sumter, African Americans in the South rallied in defense of their country. Blacks across the South were eager to fight the enemies of their homeland. Individual Southern states, and then the Confederacy, officially allowed the enlistment of free blacks at a time when the North still barred African Americans from military service.

With a rich militia tradition extending back to the War of 1812 and the American victory at Chalmette, blacks in New Orleans formed into "Native Guards" units at the war's beginning. African Americans in the East likewise came forth by the hundreds. In Petersburg, Virginia, for instance, city officials presented a Rebel banner to a large group of the town's blacks, both slave and free, who had volunteered to defend Virginia. And sixty

> "We propose [now] that we immediately commence training a large reserve of the most courageous of our slaves, and further that we guarantee freedom within a reasonable time to every slave in the South who shall remain true to the Confederacy in this war."
>
> —*General Patrick R. Cleburne*

free blacks in a newly formed volunteer company rushed to the rescue of Richmond, Virginia, in April 1861. With pride, these African Americans marched into the state capital, a Confederate banner waving at the head of their column.

Fearing amphibious landings from invading Yankees, other black Confederates rushed to defend the Atlantic coastline during the early days of the war. From Salisbury, North Carolina, more than a dozen free blacks marched east for the Atlantic coast. They were, in the words of a white Southern journalist, "in fine spirits and each wore a placard on his hat bearing the inscription 'We will die by the South.'" Also in North Carolina, an effort was made to raise "a company of free blacks [who would] be willing to turn out in behalf of our homes and friends." A short time later, blacks from the coastal islands of nearby South Carolina formed the 1st South Carolina Colored Volunteers to fight for the Union; interestingly, blacks from the Carolinas were among the first African Americans to fight in both the Union and Confederate armies.

Around this time, free African Americans in the West also began to form companies of soldiers, rallying behind their states and the new Southern nation on both sides of the Mississippi and in cities like Memphis and Nashville, Tennessee, and Fort Smith, Arkansas. However, the greatest number of African Americans joining Confederate militia ranks came from Louisiana, especially New Orleans.

As few as 50,000 Southern blacks in total served in Rebel armies, while as many as 300,000 African Americans—both slaves and free—served the Confederacy outside the armies. Quite possibly, the total number of black Confederates serving in the Southern war effort exceeded the number of African Americans serving the war effort in the North. Certainly, the Confederacy was able to

PAGE 73: A portrait of a Confederate soldier by the name of Marlborough, who served beside his owner, Randal Jones, during the entirety of the war years. ABOVE: Three black Confederate soldiers are shown here, gathered around a cooking fire at an advanced Rebel picket post outside Charleston, South Carolina. A group of white Confederate infantrymen are relaxing and playing cards nearby.

mobilize a far larger percentage of its population into the army than the Union because of the great number of African Americans living and laboring in the South.

Blacks served in Rebel armies in a variety of roles, including as musicians, servants, teamsters, laborers, cooks, and nurses. But historians seem to have forgotten another important role of African Americans in the Confederate army: combat soldier. Ironically, African Americans in the Confederate army often served side by side with whites, while in the North, though blacks might serve under white soldiers, black and white enlisted men were segregated.

For the most part, African American soldiers did not serve the Confederacy out of blind obedience, fear, or forced enrollment in Rebel armies. Black Confederates went to war to support and defend the land of their birth and to serve and fight beside the members of Southern white families. The relationship and bond between whites and blacks who had known each other since birth often transcended the traditional slave-master relationship within the military and especially on the battlefield.

The slave religion also motivated Confederate African American soldiers who believed that theirs was a righteous struggle. Black ministers inspired both white and black Confederate soldiers to do their best in battle, against all odds. From Shiloh to the war's end, one respected African American by the name of Uncle Lewis preached to the Rebels of a Tennessee regiment. After all, Confederate soldiers, black and white, were united to defend the South against the invaders who were destroying their homeland. The call to defend one's community

A young Confederate officer proudly sits for his photograph, literally side-by-side with a uniformed African American.

Jim Red was one of many black Confederates who served in defense of their Southern homeland.

and family lay behind the powerful urge to fight that was shared by both free blacks and slaves. This motivation was far more powerful for Southern blacks than for Northern blacks because the North was invaded by Rebel armies only for brief periods. Finally, just like their counterparts in blue uniforms, black Confederate soldiers in gray fought to prove that they were able to meet the challenges and trials of combat and were therefore deserving of equality.

At the war's beginning, most African Americans were assigned menial roles, with assignments in the army's rear once the fighting began. Nevertheless, many blacks did serve in the front lines, helping to save the lives of masters and the sons of masters who had been wounded. Many examples can be found of slaves rescuing their white owners in battle and caring for them in sickness. One pious African American servant named Wash emotionally wrote to "his" white family upon the death of his master, Lieutenant George Whitaker Will of the 53rd North Carolina Infantry.

> *I will now try to give you an account of my feelings towards my young master who is now dead. I hope and trust he is saved. I have reason to believe so by the light which he gave me....I am glad to tell you [that when he was buried] his coat was buttoned up in the prettiest style of uniform and in his breast pocket was his little Testament. [Before he died] we talked over everything, troubles, sorrow and sicknesses....I am willing to do anything I can do to help out our struggling country.*

This letter illustrates the deep emotional attachments that motivated many black Confederates who were "willing to do anything" to support "our struggling country."

Members of the South's "invisible army" at work: blacks strengthening the Confederate defenses and erecting fortifications on James Island, South Carolina, under the direction of General Pierre G.T. Beauregard.

Southern blacks in the Confederate army lusted for combat, and the black Rebels became involved in combat early on. As the war lengthened and manpower shortages grew more severe, more and more blacks served in the ranks at the front lines. African Americans fought' in the foremost ranks with courage and distinction, continuing the martial tradition first established during the American Revolution.

Like the French officers who were astounded to see the large percentage of blacks in Washington's ranks, one Union surgeon was shocked upon seeing General Lee's Army of Northern Virginia, the Confederacy's best army, on its way to a rendezvous with defeat at Antietam, Maryland, during the fall of 1862. The Yankee doctor noted that among the estimated sixty-four thousand Rebels pushing northward into western Maryland "over 3,000 Negroes must be included in the numbers [and] they had arms, rifles, muskets, sabers, bowie-knives, dirks, etc."

They were supplied, in many instances, with knapsacks, haversacks, canteens, etc., and they were manifestly an integral portion of the Confederate Army. They were seen riding on horses and mules, driving wagons, riding on caissons, in ambulances, with the staff of generals and promiscuously mixed up with all the Rebel horde.

Many of these African Americans who were marching north in the vain hope of

winning a decisive victory on Maryland soil would find only shallow graves along Antietam Creek. The Army of Northern Virginia was hastening to its defeat at Antietam, a loss that opened the door for Lincoln's Emancipation Proclamation. After the Battle of Antietam, Private Elbert P. Edwards, 6th New York Cavalry, wrote in disbelief of the slaughter at the "Bloody Lane," saying that it was "filled with dead Rebels [who] were all small men and many of them are very young. Their clothes are a kind of browny grey color and most terribly dirty," and that he "saw 2 dead Negroes" among the soldiers.

As the Union surgeon had observed, African Americans served even on the staffs of Confederate generals. Amos Rucker of Elbert County, Georgia, went to war with Colonel Sandy Rucker of the 33rd Georgia Infantry. In the war's beginning, he performed the typical duties of a "body servant," or valet, but that role soon developed into one more distinguished. With men dropping all around him during one hot fight, Amos picked up a musket from a fallen soldier and joined the Rebel attack. The hard-fighting Rucker remained a soldier until the end of the war, and his ability and dedication won him a coveted spot on the staff of Irish-born Major General Patrick Cleburne, "the Stonewall of the West."

Jim Lewis is the best-known African American soldier to serve on the staff of a Confederate general: Thomas J. "Stonewall" Jackson. On the battlefield, he stayed beside Stonewall while the bullets flew by in torrents. From 1861 to 1863, Lewis was the most devoted servant of the brilliant, eccentric Jackson. Lewis was so well respected by his comrades and by the Jackson family that he led the general's horse in the funeral procession after Stonewall was mortally wounded in May 1863 at Chancellorsville, Virginia.

Active military roles for African Americans in the Rebel armies were widespread at an early date. The great Frederick Douglass knew as much, and this undeniable truth deeply troubled him and other Northern blacks. In the autumn of 1861 Douglass wrote:

There are at the present moment, many colored men in the Confederate Army doing duty not only as cooks, servants, and laborers, but as real soldiers, having muskets on their shoulders and bullets in their pockets, ready to shoot down loyal troops and do all that soldiers may do to destroy the Federal government and build up that of the traitors and rebels.

Many African Americans served as drummers in Confederate units. Indeed, so many black musicians served in Rebel armies that in April 1862, the Confederate Congress officially authorized their use and made their pay equal to that of their white counterparts. In the North, meanwhile, black soldiers initially received lower pay than white Union soldiers. Henry Brown was a black Confederate who served with distinction as a drummer in the Darlington Guards, the 8th South Carolina Infantry, and then the 21st South Carolina Infantry. Born near Camden, South Carolina, in 1830, a year before Nat Turner's bloody revolt, Henry Brown was a free black who had made his living as a skilled artisan and brick mason. Another black Confederate, Mexican War veteran "Old Dick" Slate, served as the drummer of the 18th Virginia Infantry, which numbered other free black musicians in its ranks, including a fifer.

Another drummer who wore the gray was William H. Yopp. He was born in Laurens County, Georgia, in a ramshackle slave cabin on a plantation owned by one of the leading families of Georgia. He grew up

OPPOSITE: General Thomas Jonathan Jackson, General Robert E. Lee's "right arm" and top lieutenant during the most successful campaigns of the Army of Northern Virginia during 1862–1863. "Stonewall" Jackson was mortally wounded at the battle of Chancellorsville, Virginia, in May 1863. ABOVE: Portrait of Jeff Sheilds, who was Stonewall Jackson's cook during the war years and served faithfully beside the brilliant West Pointer.

TOP: African Americans supported Rebel armies by performing a wide variety of essential noncombat roles, which allowed more Confederate fighting men to serve on the front lines. BOTTOM: A shell explodes in the Confederate trenches either at Vicksburg or Port Hudson during the summer of 1863. During the forty-seven-day siege of Vicksburg, hundreds of blacks with General John C. Pemberton's army endured the dangers of the longest siege in American history up to that time.

with T.M. Yopp, the son of his master, and their relationship was, it seemed, beyond friendship—they were like brothers. When Captain T.M. Yopp went to war in the Virginia theater with the 14th Georgia Infantry, Bill Yopp went with him and their friends and neighbors. He served as the drummer for Company H and twice nursed the wounded captain back to health, saving his life during the bloody battles of the Army of Northern Virginia. When the battered Army of Northern Virginia finally surrendered at Appomattox Court House, Virginia, in April 1865, Bill Yopp was with his Georgia comrades when they laid down their arms.

The abilities of black Confederates—many of whom made instantaneous battlefield transformations from servant to soldier—were apparent in both the Confederate and the Union armies early on. In the East, for instance, one of the first Union officers killed during the war was Major Theodore Winthrop, who fell during the Battle of Big Bethel, in Virginia, in June 1861. The handsome major, who became an early Northern hero, was cut down by a shot fired by a captain's servant named Sam Ashe, a black member of the Wythe Rifles, 1st North Carolina Infantry, from Hampton, Virginia. History also remembers a cook and servant in an Alabama regiment who picked up a musket and fought at the Battle of Seven Pines during the Seven Days, in the summer of 1862.

The role of black Confederates in the West was also well-known at an early date. In early August 1861, during the "Bull Run of the West" at Wilson's Creek, Missouri, African Americans fought with General Sterling Price's frontier army. To the shock of Union soldiers, these blacks killed and wounded Federals with skillful marksmanship. And during the "Battle of Hemp Bales" at Lexington, Missouri, in mid-September 1861, Missouri blacks helped to roll the mobile hemp-bale breastworks forward to force the surrender of the surrounded Union garrison.

In both theaters of war, blacks served with distinction in Rebel artillery, cavalry, and infantry units. African Americans rode on John Hunt Morgan's raids into Kentucky and on General Nathan Bedford Forrest's slashing raids into the rear of Union armies. And numerous blacks served in the 1st South Carolina Artillery. One of these, Private John Wilson Buckner, was wounded in the defense of Fort Wagner, South Carolina, while helping to repulse the attack of the African Americans of the 54th Massachusetts. A large number of Southern blacks also served with distinction in the Confederate navy, many aboard the famous Rebel raider, the CSS *Alabama*.

During infantry attacks, black Rebels often took the initiative to pick up muskets and fight in the ranks beside white soldiers. On May 1, 1863, at Port Gibson, Mississippi, before one of the most desperate charges of the Civil War, a former slave named Shad joined the attack of the 5th Missouri Confederate Infantry. Lieutenant Colonel Robert S. Bevier of the elite 1st Missouri Confederate Brigade described how "Shad's thirst for martial glory was as pronounced as if he had been gifted with the whitest of skins."

We never went into battle that it did not require a peremptory command to keep him out; he panted for the blood of the foe [and] delighted to hear the whistle of the Minie bullet and listen to the shriek of the shrapnel. Finally he obtained consent to keep with the regiment [the 5th Missouri] in the terrific and disastrous charge we made at Port Gibson.

A photograph of three Confederate surgeons, Dr. Wilson Randolph, Dr. Kidder Taylor, and Dr. John Randolph Page, and their black body servant, Ben Harris.

There were many skilled black riflemen in the Confederate army, and their deadly work took a toll on the Union ranks, causing dismay across the Northern home front. In the tradition of Bunker Hill and Chalmette, African American marksmanship played an important role in the First Battle of Bull Run in July 1861, when a number of Federals were killed or captured by African American warriors. The harsh realization that they were fighting black Rebels came as a shock to the righteous Yankees. One Northern journalist lamented that Southern blacks "have jeered at and insulted our troops, have readily enlisted in the rebel army and on Sunday, at Manassas [in the First Battle of Bull Run],

LEFT: In this postwar portrait, Toney Wetters proudly holds close to his heart the instrument that declares his wartime identity. Wetters played the fife in the ranks of Company B, 3rd Florida Confederate Infantry. ABOVE: The South was quick to utilize talented African American marksmen, who acted as Confederate snipers. This **Harper's Weekly** *illustration depicts Union soldiers taking down one such black sniper, who had fired on Union soldiers from a tree-top hiding place.*

shot down our men with as much alacrity as if abolitionism had never existed."

The unexpected combat role of black Confederates especially dismayed the African American soldiers of the North, who were shocked to encounter blacks in Confederate gray on the battlefield. Private William H. Johnson, 2nd Connecticut, wrote in a letter of July 24, 1861, that the Southern victory at the First Battle of Bull Run "was not alone the white man's victory for it was won by slaves. Yes, the Confederates had three regiments of blacks in the field, and they maneuvered like veterans, and beat the Union men

The African Americans who worked on the fortifications of Nashville, Tennessee—albeit at bayonet-point—helped to transform it into one of the most heavily fortified cities in America.

back. This is not guessing, but it is a fact. It has angered our men, and they say there must be retaliation."

After the Seven Days battles around Richmond, a surprised Union general stated that "many men from my command were killed [by] the precision and fire of a Negro marksman, a Rebel." And in a letter from published in *Frank Leslie's* on July 12, 1863, a soldier from the Army of the Potomac reported that "a Negro serving as a sharp-shooter with the Rebel army has done more injury to our men than a dozen of his white

compeers. For some time he has been pick-ing them off from concealed positions."

The inspired fighting of the black Rebels played a role in convincing the Confederate Congress to vote for the official use of African American troops during the last six months of the war. In late February 1865, when the war was all but over, at the urging of General Lee and other Southern leaders, the Confederate Congress finally passed the "Negro Soldier Law," which allowed African Americans to enlist in black units. Had this policy of organizing African American mili-

tary commands been officially adopted by the Confederacy earlier, as it had been in the North, then the South might have held out longer, and perhaps even forced a negotiated peace. Indeed, the outcome of the Civil War was determined to a large degree by the extent to which each side successfully and thoroughly utilized its African American soldiers.

Early efforts to form Confederate black units had been thwarted. Major General Cleburne proposed the formation of black commands early in 1864. Desperate to head off an inevitable defeat, the major general wrote that "we have now been fighting for nearly three years, have spilled much of our best blood [and] our soldiers see no end to this state of affairs except in our own exhaustion." Cleburne saw that the Southerner's only solution was to give "up the negro slaves rather than be a slave himself." Hence, he had proposed the formation of black units that would allow slaves to fight for their freedom. But his proposal had been rejected.

When the Confederate Congress finally acted on Cleburne's proposal, the general was unable to be around to celebrate this victory—he had died in the holocaust at Franklin, Tennessee, in late November 1864. And by now it was too late to rescue the dying Confederacy, even with the aid of black units.

Colonel William C. Oates, the hard-fighting commander of the 15th Alabama

With Federal troops situated throughout the South, many Southerners feared that slaves could easily escape into Federal territory. The movement of slaves became restricted by the formation of a home guard, also known as plantation police.

Infantry, which had almost captured Little Round Top at Gettysburg on July 2, 1863, viewed this delay as one of the great lost opportunities of the war. The colonel maintained that thousands of blacks could have been easily transformed into Confederate soldiers.

The bonds of friendship between white boys and negroes were strong [and these] negroes were the last hope for Confederate recruits, and it was then too late [and] had the law been passed two years earlier the Confederacy could have raised and kept in the field three hundred thousand negro soldiers [and] the world in arms never could have conquered us. …If at Gettysburg Lee had 50,000 negro troops under white officers, as additional force, he would have walked over [General George] Meade's army, have gone to Philadelphia and peace would then have been made.

However, Union Sergeant Thomas B. Webster, 43rd United States Colored Infantry, held a far different view. In a December 1864 letter, Sergeant Webster wrote with disgust:

[The South has] exhausted the material to organize new white armies, and they now, as a last resource, call upon the black men of the South—the poor, despised, down trodden slaves—to fight against the glorious Union [and now] they call upon the black men to do what they themselves have not been able to do. But will the slave fight against us? Will he fight against his own father, son, or brother, now in arms for universal liberty and the preservation of this glorious Union? No, never!

George Johnson, from Virginia's Shenandoah Valley, was the body servant of the famous Confederate cavalry commander General Turner Ashby until the general's death in battle in June 1862.

The Forgotten Role of African American Women in the Civil War

The forgotten participants of the African American experience during the Civil War were indisputably black women. Indeed, even in peacetime, African American women had played a key role as the anchor of black community and family life, continuing the matriarchal traditions of West African societies. Historians, however, have too often overlooked the important role of African American women, especially during the Civil War.

While African American men were off at war, these women compensated for their absence by working harder and taking on more responsibilities, including secular and spiritual leadership roles within their communities and on plantations across the South, than ever before. Their wartime role was essentially the same as that of white Southern women during the years of the Civil War. Like the men they raised, supported, and sent off to the war, African American women endured their own share of sacrifice and suffering from 1861 to 1865.

The roles of black women often extended beyond their

Harriet Tubman, "the Moses of her people," is perhaps the most celebrated heroine—black or white—of the Civil War era. Shown here in later years with some of the hundreds of ex-slaves she guided to freedom, Tubman (far left) risked capture and a return to slavery during nearly twenty journeys along the invisible Underground Railroad.

own families and communities. During the four years of war, African American women assisted Union armies across the South as spies, nurses, couriers, cooks, laundresses, laborers, and so on. Black nurses served with both the Union armies and the Union navy.

Across the South during the four years of war, escaped Union prisoners were assisted by black women who gave food, clothes, directions, and comfort to Union soldiers. Many of these unknown black heroines risked all to assist escaped prisoners and Union forces across the South.

Perhaps the best known black woman of the Civil War era was Harriet Tubman, twice a fugitive. In 1849, Tubman escaped slavery for good, as well as a marriage forced upon her by the plantation owner. A friend of the notorious John Brown, Tubman was the most famous agent of the Underground Railroad, which led from the South to stretch across Ohio and Indiana in the West and across New York and New England in the East. Risking a return to slavery—there was a fouty-thousand-dollar reward for her capture—courageous Tubman was known as the "Moses of her people." She led hundreds of slaves to freedom during nearly twenty dangerous journeys along the invisible tracks of the Underground Railroad that led fugitives such as Frederick Douglass northward to the land of freedom, Canada.

During the Civil War, Tubman, who never learned to read or write, supported the Federal presence in South Cartolina as a nurse, laundress, and spy. After the war Tubman told her biographer, "I started with this idea in my head, 'There's two things I've got a right to…death or liberty.'" Frederick Douglass wrote to her, on August 29, 1868: "Excepting John Brown—of sacred memory—I know of no one who had willingly encountered more perils and hardships to serve our enslaved people than you have." Yet Tubman was only one of thousands of gallant African American women in both the North and South who made sacrifices and risked freedom, physical punishment, and death for their beliefs while serving as the sturdy pillars of African American community and social life, both slave and free.

chapter 5

HEROISM UNDER FIRE

The Emancipation Proclamation, combined with the repeal of the 1792 militia law prohibiting blacks from service and the changed attitudes among both military and government leaders in the North, opened the floodgates to black recruits who were eager to fight for themselves and for the country that had set them free.

These black Union soldiers were highly motivated to defeat the South, where family members remained in bondage and the terrible legacy of slavery was intact. The war was a struggle to preserve newly won freedom and to exterminate the institution of slavery. With his call to arms, Frederick Douglass implored African Americans across the land to come forth and play a role in wiping slavery off the North American continent once and for all: "I urge you to fly to arms and smite with death the power that would bury the government and your liberty in the same hopeless grave." Such emotional appeals

were not in vain. Tens of thousands of African Americans poured into the Union army and navy, eager for the chance to serve their country and to prove their worth as fighting men.

Thirty thousand black seamen, an estimated one-fourth of the entire Union navy, served on the waters of the oceans and in the Gulf of Mexico. Unlike the army, the Union navy had imposed no racial barriers to black enlistment from the war's beginning—men of any color, origin, or ethnic background could become seamen. African Americans served on the high seas with an equality that was absent on land. During the four years of war, blacks in navy uniforms served as gunners, pilots, and seamen on gunships and aboard the blockade fleet ringing the coastlines of the Southern states. During the Civil War, eight African Americans of the Union navy won the Congressional Medal of Honor for outstanding valor.

"The bravery of the blacks in the battle of Milliken's Bend completely revolutionized the sentiment of the Army with regard to the employment of Negro troops."

—Charles Dana

On land, however, African Americans first had to demonstrate to Northern whites, the government, and fellow soldiers that they were indeed as capable of fighting hard as whites. From the beginning of the war to the end, African Americans would accomplish this with courage and heroism. The contributions of the black soldiery were so crucial to the war effort that in 1864 President Lincoln admitted without exaggeration that the services of African Americans absolutely had to be retained in Union ranks to see the war through to its successful conclusion: "Keep it and you can save the Union [but] throw it away, and the Union goes with it."

African Americans yearned to demonstrate their worth as individuals and to prove their ability to endure the same dangers and challenges as white soldiers. Hence, blacks fought and died with frightful frequency,

just like the thousands of white soldiers who had been slaughtered year after year. Only by advancing in long lines against entrenched Southern troops or by repulsing Confederate attacks would African American courage be proved. Only with black sacrifice and heroism on the battlefield could equality be demonstrated to silence critics who proclaimed that the slave was undeserving of citizenship. If black soldiers won a decisive victory for the hard-pressed Union during its greatest hour of need, equality on the home front could no longer be denied in the name of the alleged inferiority of African Americans.

Of course, the question of black combat capabilities should have been a moot point because African American courage had already been proved again and again throughout the annals of American military

history. African American performances on the battlefields of the past—from the American Revolution to the dread slave revolts of the antebellum period—had already demonstrated the fitness of African Americans to fully meet the many challenges of combat as readily and as well as white troops. But because of prejudice on the part of the white men already enjoying the benefits of full citizenship, Northerners had yet to be convinced of these long-proven realities. Significantly, the realities of black valor on the battlefield also had to be demonstrated to the new generation of African Americans recently out of bondage. With so much at stake, it is no wonder that black soldiers were eager to demonstrate their abilities, not only to themselves but also to other Americans, both black and white.

However, the people of the American nation finally had the opportunity to read many glowing reports and learn of the fighting skill and spirit of African Americans after a little-known engagement at Milliken's Bend, Louisiana, in June 1863. This seemingly obscure engagement along the Mississippi River, also taking place in the Trans-Mississippi, was in fact quite important in strategic terms, for much was at stake at Milliken's Bend.

The Battle of Milliken's Bend was part of the struggle for the strategically important fortress of Vicksburg, the key to the West and perhaps to the outcome of the war itself. Milliken's Bend lay only a short distance northwest of Vicksburg, across the Mississippi River in eastern Louisiana. The location of Milliken's Bend and its proximity to Vicksburg made the fight for this strategic position significant. The Battle of Milliken's Bend resulted from an attempt by the South to capture this Mississippi River outpost, which was an important link between the resource-rich Trans-Mississippi and the eastern part of the Confederacy.

PAGE 89: Soldiers of the 107th United States Colored Troops in formation before the guardhouse at Fort Corcoran, on the heights of Arlington, Virginia, on the west side of the Potomac River. ABOVE: Down the same New York City streets that witnessed the violence of the draft riots of 1863, black soldiers of the 20th United States Colored Troops march to war.

Drivers of the baggage train of General Alfred Pleasanton's cavalry brigade, Army of the Potomac, watering their horses in the Rappahannock River in central Virginia.

African Americans in the Union Navy

The tradition of African American service in the navies of the United States stretched as far back as the founding of the American republic. Indeed, blacks served and fought with distinction on naval vessels and privateers during the American Revolution. Afterward, thousands of black seamen served side-by-side with white sailors in the wars against the Barbary pirates, the War of 1812, and during the Seminole and Mexican wars. In the decades before the Civil War, life on the high seas offered a rare avenue of equality on the high seas for blacks that was not available to them as civilians in either the North or the South.

Compared to other branches of the armed forces, duty in the Union navy provided both the earliest and the greatest opportunity for blacks to serve their country. This equal opportunity in the navy began early in the Civil War. The navy was

The crew of the famous USS Monitor on the James River outside Richmond, Virginia, in July 1862. The clash between the USS Monitor and the CSS Merrimack, in March 1862, remains one of the most famous naval duels in history.

authorized to enlist "contra-band"—fugitive or liberated ex-slaves—in late September 1861, less than six months after the firing on Fort Sumter. Serving on the rivers, bayous, and oceans, nearly thirty thousand African Americans, comprising one-fourth of the navy, compiled a distinguished record from 1861 to 1865.

Familiar with the waterways of the South, some black men such as Robert Smalls, an ex-slave from Charleston, South Carolina, served as pilots of United States naval vessels. In May 1862 and before joining the navy, Smalls earned widespread

RIGHT: John Lawson, a landsman in the Union navy, won the Congressional Medal of Honor for valor during the battle of Mobile Bay, Alabama, August 5, 1864, while serving on Admiral David Farragut's flag-ship, the USS Hartford.
BELOW: Taking advantage of the absence of the Confederate cap-tain, Robert Smalls (right), a former South Carolina slave, captured the Rebel steamer Planter (left) and piloted it past Fort Sumter and out of the har-bor of Charleston, South Carolina, to reach the safety of the Federal blockading fleet on May 12, 1862.

Robert Smalls.

recognition for capturing and running the steamer *Planter* past the guns of Fort Sumter and out of Charleston harbor to the safety of the nearby blockading fleet of Union warships. Smalls then served as the pilot of the *Planter* in the blockading fleet outside Southern port cities.

Most important, blacks in the Union navy fought in an integrated service, unlike in Northern armies. Eight black sailors won Medals of Honor for heroism during the Civil War. In 1864, winners of the Medal of Honor were Robert Blake, William Henry Brown, Wilson Brown, Clement Dees, John Lawson, James Mifflin, an engineer's cook who rose to the challenge, and Joachim Pease. The only black naval winner of the nation's highest award for valor during the final year of war, Aaron Anderson won the Medal of Honor in 1865. In the more egalitarian service of the navy, these African Americans won the Medal of Honor long before their counterparts in the armies of the North were so honored.

More than thirty black crewmen, both young and old, pose aboard the USS Vermont *in the waters off Hilton Head, South Carolina, in 1863.*

An African American corporal prepared for action with his Colt revolver across his chest. Many of the black troops fighting in the Southern states were staking their freedom as well as their lives.

The mighty fortress of Vicksburg on the east bank of the Mississippi was besieged by an immense army under General Grant. General Joseph E. Johnston's Confederate army, which was situated east of Vicksburg, failed to come to the city's relief. Nor was relief forthcoming from the Confederacy's primary eastern army under General Lee. Earlier, Lee had convinced the Confederate president, Jefferson Davis, to send the Army of Northern Virginia northward to invade Pennsylvania during the summer of 1863 instead of sending Rebel troops west to reinforce Vicksburg. And finally, General Braxton Bragg in the west would not strike a blow or send reinforcements to relieve the dying thirty-thousand-man garrison at Vicksburg, which had been abandoned to its own fate. The only hope for the surrounded Rebel garrison, bottled up for weeks on the Mississippi, was from outside relief by way of the Trans-Mississippi. It was up to the Trans-Mississippi Rebels to come to Vicksburg's rescue.

In early 1863, therefore, Confederate General John G. Walker, a Mexican War veteran from Missouri, prepared to relieve Vicksburg by capturing Milliken's Bend, located on the west bank of the Mississippi. The Confederate leadership hoped that the capture of Milliken's Bend would disrupt Grant's supply line and break up the siege of Vicksburg. Ironically, however, Grant's army had already employed this bayou country of eastern Louisiana in moving down the Mississippi's east bank to eventually cross the river below Vicksburg, launching the greatest amphibious operation of the war. Unknown to Confederate planners, that supply route and logistical support system on the west side of the Mississippi no longer existed for Grant's besieging army. Grant's logistical line had been transferred to the Mississippi's east side, running down to the Mississippi River base site at Grand Gulf, Mississippi.

At the quiet outpost of Milliken's Bend, meanwhile, more than one thousand African Americans, the majority of the small garrison, made a name for themselves despite having seen no prior combat. With their backs to the Mississippi and no escape available, the 9th and 11th United States Colored regiments tenaciously withstood the ferocious attack of General Walker's forty-five-hundred-man division of battle-hardened Texans. After the howling Texas Confederates overran the Union encampment, the African Americans fought hand-to-hand during some of the most savage combat of the war. Against the odds, black and white Yankees repulsed the Rebel effort to capture Milliken's Bend.

This bloody Louisiana engagement along the Mississippi made a significant impact, allowing blacks the opportunity to prove that

In the face of a fierce attack by Texas Rebels during the battle of Milliken's Bend, Louisiana, African Americans struggle in hand-to-hand combat. Their counterattack drove back the Confederates, thereby ensuring General Grant's successful reduction of Vicksburg.

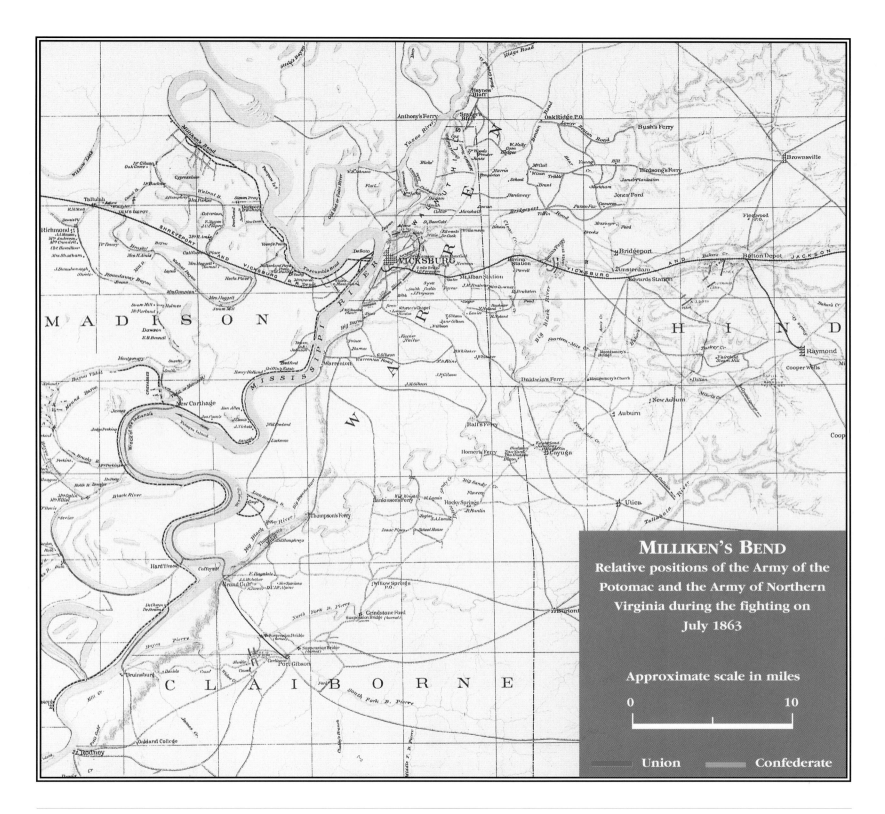

MILLIKEN'S BEND

Relative positions of the Army of the Potomac and the Army of Northern Virginia during the fighting on July 1863

Approximate scale in miles

0   10

Union   Confederate

they were indeed dependable, hard-fighting soldiers who could stand up to the greatest challenges on the battlefield. Their actions drew notice; as Lincoln's assistant secretary of war, Charles Dana, now emphasized, "The bravery of the blacks in the battle of Milliken's Bend completely revolutionized the sentiment of the Army with regard to the employment of Negro troops."

Likewise impressed by the spirited resistance of the African Americans in blue at Milliken's Bend was General Grant, who had needed that dramatic victory. The repulse of the Southerners at Milliken's Bend was necessary because Grant had to dispel the threat from west of the Mississippi to ensure the capture of Vicksburg. Thanks in part to the

capability of the African Americans who successfully defended Milliken's Bend, Grant's siege of Vicksburg continued unabated, choking the life out of the encircled city throughout the spring of 1863. Partly as a result of the unexpected victory at Milliken's Bend, the fall of the fortress city on July 4, 1863—a decisive turning point in the war— was all but inevitable.

The engagement that first and most forcefully demonstrated the combat prowess of black troops in offensive operations was not at the now-better-publicized charge of the 54th Massachusetts at Fort Wagner, South Carolina, in July 1863. Rather, widespread recognition of black courage first came during the siege of Port Hudson, Louisiana.

ABOVE: The Colored Soldiers' Hospital in Beaufort, South Carolina, November 1864. RIGHT: Soldiers recently recovered from wounds and illness at Aiken's Landing, Virginia, on the James River in 1864.

By the summer of 1863, only two Confederate strong points along the Mississippi remained to defend the great river—Vicksburg and Port Hudson. After Vicksburg's fall on the Fourth of July, the Confederacy was all but cut in two, but the fortified bastion of Port Hudson had to be taken before the Union could win complete control of the Mississippi. With the massive fortifications of Port Hudson arrayed along the river bluffs on the east side of "the Father of Waters," the challenge was formidable.

Here, on the banks of the Mississippi, the forces under Union General Nathaniel P. Banks besieged Port Hudson and its garrison of six thousand Rebel troops under the command of New York–born General Franklin Gardner, a West Pointer and Mexican War veteran. Much like the fortress of Vicksburg, the strongly fortified Port Hudson dominated the high ground overlooking the great river. But the isolated stronghold was surrounded by a tight ring of thousands of Yankees, and the siege of Port Hudson began to strangle the life out of the garrison. Like Grant at the beginning of Vicksburg's forty-seven-day siege, Banks was impatient for both political and domestic reasons, and he envisioned a quick victory rather than a long siege.

Consequently, on May 27, a confident General Banks ordered frontal assaults to carry the powerful fortifications by storm. Though insufficiently trained and new at the business of soldiering, the hardy African Americans of the 1st Louisiana Native Guards were given the tough assignment of assaulting some of the strongest fortifications at Port Hudson. This regiment, including its line officers, unlike other black units, consisted of free blacks of French Creole ancestry with last names such as Calloux, Porée, Orillion,

A February 1865 impressment receipt and "appraisement certificate" for a slave named Thomas, age twenty-two.

RECEIPT.

RECEIVED of *Geo N Sims* of *Jefferson* county, one slave named *Thomas*, aged *22*, color *Black*, height *5 ft. 5"* weight *150* appraised at *forty five hundred* dollars, impressed this *9* day of *February*, A. D. 186*5*, under the act of Congress, approved February 17, 1864, "To increase the efficiency of the army by the enrollment of Free Negroes and Slaves in certain capacities," and to be employed for the purposes therein specified, and who is to be returned at the expiration of twelve months from the date of impressment at *Monticello*

J. P. Saunderson Impressing Agent.

CERTIFICATE OF APPRAISEMENT.

WE, the undersigned, chosen by *J. P. Saunderson* agent on the one part, and by *D. H. Hoge agt* on the other part, first being duly sworn, do this *9* day of *February*, 186*5*, appraise and value the slave described in the foregoing receipt at *forty five hundred* dollars. *& Clothing $. 20* *Total $. 4520* Witness our hands and seals.

The above appraisement is } *Appd* *J. Saunderson* *Imp Agt* *Geo W Taylor* [L. S.] [L. S.] *E. H. Willie* [L. S.] Umpire.

SURGEONS' CERTIFICATE.

The Board of Surgeons for the examination of Conscripts for the *Second* Congressional District do hereby certify that we have carefully examined the slave named in the foregoing receipt and find him sound, able-bodied and fit for the required service.

February 9 186 *5* *Elihu Foland* } Surgeons.

NEGRO IMPRESSMENT RECEIPT AND APPRAISEMENT CERTIFICATE DURING THE CIVIL WAR

ABOVE: Born in 1837 in Mali, Africa, where he was captured by Arab slave traders, Nicholas Saib was a teacher in Detroit, Michigan, before he enlisted to fight for the Union. He served in the ranks of the 55th Massachusetts Volunteer Infantry, which served in South Carolina. RIGHT: A number of United States Colored troops in winter quarters at an unnamed Union encampment in the South. BELOW: An African American soldier named Johnson was hanged on June 20, 1864, for allegedly raping a white woman.

Lavigne, and St. Louis. The 3rd Louisiana Native Guards, consisting primarily of former slaves commanded by white officers, were also ordered to attack the fortifications of Port Hudson. The formidable defenses on the Confederate left of Port Hudson's fortified line were the imposing target of these black soldiers of Colonel John A. Nelson's brigade, General William Dwight's division, on the Federal right wing.

During the bloody morning of May 27, more than one thousand African Americans assaulted the seemingly impregnable Confederate earthworks in obsolete Napoleonic attack formations, without support and across rough, open, and flooded terrain—a certain recipe for disaster. The black soldiers did as ordered—they advanced in the doomed assault with cheers, bugles blaring, and flags flying. The attackers suffered terribly under brutal frontal fire and enfilade, men falling all around from volleys of musketry and blasts of canister. Black color sergeants dropped to rise no more, but other soldiers picked up the blood-soaked banners and continued onward through the hail of projectiles, encouraging their comrades forward in the din.

With the 1st Louisiana Native Guards leading the way, the charging African Americans continued their advance through the storm of lead. These blacks charged across hundreds of yards of rugged terrain while a solid sheet of fire from musketry and artillery rained down upon them from the ridge covered with veteran Mississippi infantrymen and rows of booming artillery. The assault of the African Americans at Port Hudson was heroic, but suicidal.

Casualties were high among the African American attackers. The 3rd Louisiana Native

African American troops attacking the powerful defenses of Port Hudson, Louisiana, fighting hand-to-hand with the defenders along the parapet.

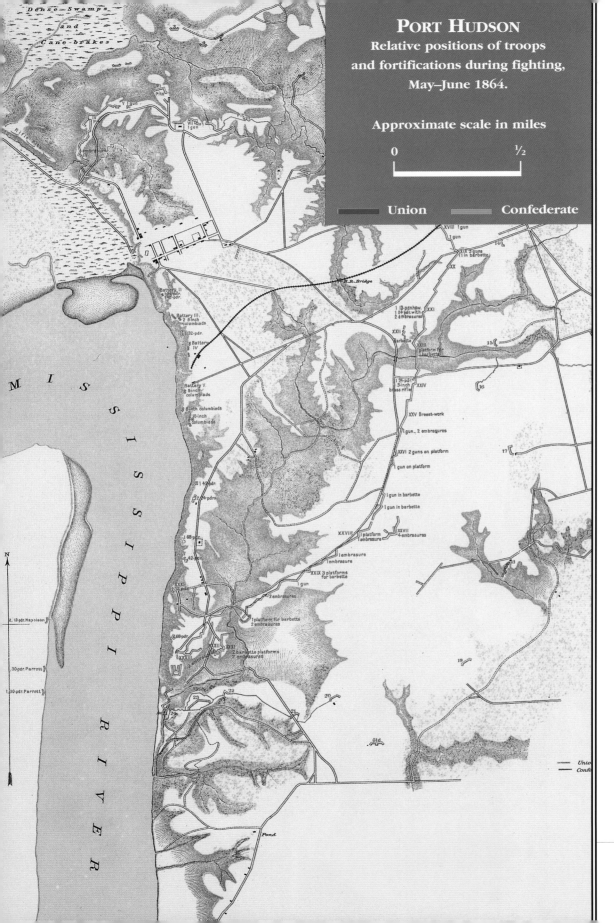

PORT HUDSON

Relative positions of troops
and fortifications during fighting,
May–June 1864.

Approximate scale in miles

0   ½

Union   Confederate

Guards suffered the highest percentage of losses among Banks' black troops on May 27. The staggering casualty count of this single black regiment during this brief attack was 308: 37 killed, 155 wounded, and another 116 missing. The price of glory had been high during the bloody assaults on the fortress of Port Hudson.

Also on May 27, as part of the same effort to take Port Hudson, the 1st Louisiana Native Guards Engineers launched another desperate attack that no one would ever forget. The African American troops led the way across the open killing fields before an array of massive fortifications. Unlike their comrades in the 3rd Louisiana Native Guards, however, these soldiers went forward without weapons. Instead they carried wooden poles to bridge the deep ditch at the base of the formidable network of fortifications. As elsewhere along the attacking line on that bloody day, this courageous attempt by black troops only resulted in the slaughter of the attackers.

Like most frontal assaults during this war, including General Grant's doomed attacks on Vicksburg on May 19 and 22, Banks' attempt to storm Port Hudson's fortifications on May 27 was a disaster. African American soldiers paid a high price for the tactical blunder and overconfidence of the commanding general. Even worse, the bloody lessons of May 27 were ignored, for on June 14, an impatient General Banks once again sent thousands of infantrymen across the open fields to attack the powerful fortifications of Port Hudson, and once again the men were slaughtered.

Union General Daniel Ullmann summarized the distinguished role and high sacrifice of the attacking black soldiers at Port Hudson. "The troops made six or seven charges over this ground against the enemy's works," he wrote. "They were exposed to a terrible fire and were dreadfully slaughtered

Drilling by the gun crews of a battery of the "Corps d'Afrique" at Port Hudson, Louisiana.

[but] all who witnessed these charges . . . agree that their conduct was such as would do honor to any soldier." Not long after Vicksburg's capture, after a six-week siege, Port Hudson finally fell, giving the Union complete control of the Mississippi. With considerable pride, General Banks declared that the heroism demonstrated by his black soldiers during their attacks on Port Hudson forever "settles the question that the negro race can fight with great prowess."

The distinguished combat of black soldiers at Milliken's Bend and Port Hudson succeeded in helping General Grant to achieve his great goal of conquering the Mississippi River for the Union. The impressive performance of African Americans was not forgotten by the gifted Western general who would later capture Richmond and accept General Lee's surrender at Appomattox. On his rapid rise to top commander of the Union forces, Grant became a forceful and influential advocate of black soldiers, unlike many of his less enlightened

General Ulysses S. Grant, the architect of decisive Union victory, was a high-level supporter of African American troops, understanding that these soldiers, fighting for their own freedom, would prove crucial to winning the war.

> *"By arming the Negro we have added a powerful ally. They will make good soldiers and taking them from the enemy weakens him in the same proportion they strengthen us. I am therefore most decidedly in favor of pushing this policy...."*
>
> —General Ulysses S. Grant

and less visionary peers. With a clear understanding of the brutal arithmetic that would separate winner from loser in this war of attrition, Grant assured President Lincoln that "by arming the Negro we have added a powerful ally. They will make good soldiers and taking them from the enemy weakens him in the same proportion they strengthen us. I am therefore most decidedly in favor of pushing this policy."

But the accomplishments of African Americans in the armed forces did not stop with their valor at Port Hudson. Thousands of black soldiers in Union ranks were performing far beyond the expectations of both military and civilian leaders. Colonel

Higginson, leading the 1st South Carolina Volunteers on expeditions into the hostile regions of Georgia and Florida, analyzed the determination that led to the many impressive accomplishments of his black soldiery. "Perhaps the best proof of a good average of courage among them," he wrote, "was in the readiness they always showed for any special enterprise [for I never] had the slightest difficulty in obtaining volunteers, but rather of keeping down the number."

Colonel Higginson summarized the various factors that made the African American soldiers especially effective in combat, even more so than white troops in some respects, as follows:

No doubt there were reasons why this particular war was an especially

Doing his duty, an African American guard challenges the cigar-smoking General Grant, the highest-ranking Union commander in the North. This incident was well publicized to illustrate the high discipline of black troops. Here, the guard, a mere private, curtly gives an order to General Grant, "You must throw away that cigar, Sir!" before allowing him to enter a commissary warehouse.

favorable test of the colored soldiers. They had more to fight for than the whites. Besides the flag and the Union, they had home and wife and child. They fought with ropes round their necks, and when orders were issued that the officers of colored troops should be put to death on capture, they took a grim satisfaction. It helped their esprit de corps immensely. With us, at least, there was to be no play-soldier [because] in case of ultimate defeat, the northern troops, black or white, would go home, while the First South Carolina must fight it out or be re-enslaved.

Another factor that contributed to the high morale, resolve, and fierce fighting spirit of these black troops was their strong,

African American Soldiers at the Battle of the Crater

One of the most famous Civil War engagements in which African American troops fought was the bloody Battle of the Crater at Petersburg, below Richmond, Virginia, in late July 1864. In an attempt to break the stalemate at Petersburg, a regiment of Pennsylvania coal miners, without the assistance of the Army of the Potomac's engineers, dug a 511-foot (155.8m) mine under a Confederate strong point along the Petersburg line. For this novel enterprise, the Keystone Staters had obtained the approval of General Burnside, who was anxious to redeem his

RIGHT: In well-aligned attack formations with fixed bayonets and flags flying, the soldiers of the 22nd United States Colored Infantry charge across open terrain to attack a high-ground defensive position at Petersburg, Virginia, on June 16, 1864. BELOW: Sharpened logs create a formidable obstacle, known as chevaux-de-frise, which were encountered by the 22nd United States Colored Infantry during its attack on the fortifications of Petersburg.

reputation after his Fredericksburg disaster in late 1862, and General Grant, who wanted to end the war in one stroke. Once the mine was completed, more than eight thousand (3,632kg) pounds of black powder would be emplaced forty feet (12.2m) under the Rebel position along the Petersburg defensive line known as Elliott's Salient. This key defensive sector was held by the Confederate brigade of General Stephen Elliott, Jr., for whom the salient was named.

On July 23, a soldier of the 48th Pennsylvania Volunteer Infantry, the regiment responsible for digging the mine, wrote to his uncle and bragged how these Pennsylvania soldiers of the IX Corps "have projected, undertaken, and completed a gigantic work, and have accomplished one of the greatest things in this war [and have] excavated a mine gallery from our line to and under the enemy's works. This mine is 511 feet [155.8m] in length, and has lateral galleries of 75 feet [22.9m], making a total distance of 586 feet [178.6m]. I am [now] under one of their principal forts, and as soon as the 'high

General Ambrose E. Burnside ordered his IX Corps into the depths of the crater, repeating the folly of his suicidal frontal assaults on Fredericksburg in December 1862 as the commander of the Army of the Potomac.

The great mine explosion at Petersburg created a huge crater, while Union artillery simultaneously opened fire so that onrushing Federal infantrymen—both black and white—could exploit the breach in the Confederate lines.

authorities' are ready, will put 12,000 (twelve thousand) lbs. [5,448kg] of [black] powder in 9 enormous magazines and will blow fort, cannon, and rebels to the clouds." After much effort, the mine was finally completed and scheduled to explode at the end of July. The giant blast was calculated by Union leaders to set in action a brilliant plan to break the stalemate and perhaps end the war.

On July 30, thousands of soldiers of General Burnside's IX Corps stood in position to exploit the long-awaited break in the lines. The plan was for these veteran troops to charge through the hole blown into the Confederate lines. A supporter and friend of black troops, General Burnside had originally selected his African American division—under General Edward Ferrero—to lead the IX Corps' assault through the Confederate lines after the mine's explosion to open the way to Petersburg, the most strategic city in the Confederacy. Such a success would result in the decisive defeat of General Robert E. Lee's Army of Northern Virginia, splitting that legendary army in half. The African Americans of the 4th Division were eager for the challenge, desiring to prove their worth not only to the Army of the Potomac, but to the entire nation.

However, the original plan of attack was altered when concerns arose among some Union

Thousands of troops of the IX Corps surge forward on bloody July 30, 1864, pouring into the crater that would become a death trap.

leaders that they would be open to charges of racism should they employ this lone African American regiment to lead the charge as "cannon fodder." Consequently, and much to the disappointment of the African Americans in blue, a white division of Burnside's corps was now chosen to lead the dangerous attack instead of the black 4th Division.

During the early morning hours of a humid and hot July 30, the huge mine was exploded beneath the 250 unfortunate South Carolina soldiers manning Elliott's Salient, blowing up the defenders and creating a wide crater in the Confederate line. Rebel defenders, artillery, and tons of earth ascended skyward in a thundering cloud that rose a hundred feet (30.5m) into the air. Seemingly, with the sunrise of July 30, a wide and open path was now blown in the Petersburg line for the IX Corps to advance through and capture Petersburg.

However, the IX Corps' assault to exploit the break in the Southern line began belatedly, after sunrise, allowing the Rebels time to recover from the shock of the great blast and rally. The Confederates had been expecting the mine's explosion for weeks and had established a second defensive line behind Elliott's Salient. Finally, the Federal attack was

Veteran Confederates of General William Mahone's brigade counterattack to push the Federals out of the embattled crater, where intermingled groups of black and white bluecoats resist the assault with bayonets and musket-butts.

launched, and thousands of bluecoats surged toward the demolished line at the partly destroyed salient. Twenty-two African American regiments of General Ferrero's 4th Division charged toward the smoking crater, attacking behind the onrushing white units of General Burnside's IX Corps.

One of the charging black regiments was the 39th Colored Infantry, which was composed of soldiers from Baltimore, Maryland, the northernmost coastal city of the South. During the struggle for the crater, Sergeant Decatur Dorsey would win the Medal of Honor for planting the colors of the 39th

Colored Infantry on the Confederate works to inspire his comrades to continue the advance in the face of a blistering fire.

In anticipation of the mine explosion and in good firing positions to counter the advantage gained by the attackers, carefully placed Confederate

batteries to the salient's rear opened a heavy fire as the confident mass of Federals surged into the crater. Additionally, reinforced Southern troops rallied on either side of the crater opened fire on the exposed flanks of the IX Corps.

Under a scorching fire, some ten thousand IX Corps

Engᵈ by Augustus Robin, N.Y.

General Edward Ferrero was the leader of the all-black 4th Division of Burnside's IX Corps. Although his troops were originally slated to lead the charge into the crater, the plan was altered when concerns arose among Union leaders that they would be open to charges of racism should they send this lone African American brigade on such a potentially suicidal mission.

Yankees were massed in and around the crater, stalling the advance as the assault's momentum came to a halt. Instead of advancing on either side of the crater to widen the narrow breach in the Rebel lines, the Federals remained mostly in the crater, losing the initiative. Lacking inspired commanders to lead the troops forward and exploit the Union's advantage, the seemingly befuddled IX Corps—in a repeat of the repulses before Burnside's Bridge at Antietam on September 17, 1862—failed to advance in force beyond the crater, as three precious hours passed and chances for success slipped away.

Nevertheless, the African Americans of Ferrero's division proved themselves to be "dusky heroes" during the bloody struggle around the crater, fighting and dying beside the white soldiers of Burnside's ill-fated IX Corps. Ordered to capture the high ground of Cemetery Hill beyond the crater, one black brigade of Ferrero's division surged forward, attacking out of the crater. Although denied the opportunity to lead the IX Corps' assault because of Union leadership's fear of high casualties and the resulting political repercussions from the disproportionate sacrifice, the African Americans were now leading the attack beyond the crater

HEROISM UNDER FIRE

with even less chance for success now that the Confederates had rallied.

While most white units of the IX Corps remained around the crater, one 48th Pennsylvania soldier never forgot the sight of the valiant assault of the African Americans who boldly attacked Cemetery Hill, after surging from the depths of the hellish crater:

By nine o'clock in the morning, the Confederates [had] collected their senses and proceeded to pour into that crater such a hell of artillery fire as the world has never seen. They raked the hill on both sides with rifle fire, until no living being could stand against it. The poor colored troops were finally led out and up the hill. They charged, some through, some to the right [or northwest] of the crater; but on they went straight into the inferno before them, yelling and shouting [but] suddenly there rose before them a wall of gray-clad figures with bayonets [and shortly] the crest had been retaken.

Attackers of the IX Corps plunge into the hell of the smoking crater, surging forward with renewed vigor to exploit the break in the lines of Petersburg.

All the while, more African American soldiers at the crater fell to the ceaseless fires of both Southern artillery and musketry during the brutal struggle for possession of the crater. Along with white soldiers, some of these hard-hit black troops fell back in confusion to escape the fury of the counterattack of General William "Billy" Mahone's Georgia and Virginia Division and the escalating slaughter. Enraged by the sight of black troops on the battlefield, counterattacking Rebels killed some black soldiers who surrendered and fell into their hands, including some wounded.

Facing an uncertain situation on this battlefield, some white United States Colored Infantry officers were at risk of retaliation from revenge-seeking Rebels during the hand-to-hand fighting that swirled around the crater. When captured, some of these white officers denied their association with the United States Colored Infantry to save themselves. Worst of all, a number of black soldiers fell to the fire of other Yankees. For instance, racist infantrymen of a Western regiment, wrote one Federal, "deliberately shot down many of the retreating [black] soldiers [and the casualties steadily mounted among the] dusky heroes" of Petersburg.

On bloody July 30, Union leaders were unable to meet the challenges of the struggle for the crater, failing to provide the leadership necessary to successfully exploit the break in General Lee's line. Therefore, the soldiers of the IX Corps, both black and white, fought largely on their own hook, holding their advanced and vulnerable positions around the crater while more Rebels counterattacked. Additional Southern artillery, including lethal mortars that lobbed shells into the crater, pounded the Yankees who stubbornly held the body-strewn crater, and died for their tenacity.

Union ambitions for exploiting the break in the Confederate lines ended forever as thousands of battle-hardened Virginia and Georgia infantrymen of Mahone's division hurled the Yankees, both black and white, from the crater. From beginning to end, the Battle of the Crater was simply another bloody disaster for the Army of the Potomac. Nearly four thousand soldiers of the Army of the Potomac fell in a futile attempt to break the Petersburg stalemate. Once again, Union leadership had failed to match the fighting prowess of the men in the ranks, resulting in yet another defeat and thousands of casualties for no gain.

Nevertheless, a measure of hard-earned glory was won by the black troops of the IX Corps during the bloody Battle of the

Crater, despite this having been their first engagement. One African American brigade of General Ferrero's division, for example, lost 1,324 soldiers, which was 35 percent of the total casualties suffered by the Army of the Potomac during the Battle of the Crater. Glory had come at a frightfully high cost.

The 29th United States Colored Infantry entered the fight on July 30 with 450 soldiers, and lost 322 men during the furious struggle. Shocked by the length of the casualty list and yet another setback for his Army of the Potomac, General Grant merely concluded with regret how the crater disaster was "the saddest affair" that he had seen during the four years of war. As a measure of their valor and the extent of their disproportionate sacrifice, the black troops suffered 40 percent of the fatalities inflicted upon the Army of the Potomac on bloody July 30.

RIGHT: General Ulysses S. Grant was the conqueror in the West, including Vicksburg, who came east to lead the Army of the Potomac to decisive victory during the campaigns of 1864–65, thanks in no small part to the efforts and sacrifices of thousands of black troops. FAR RIGHT: The soldiers of Company E, 4th United States Colored Troops, who served with distinction in the Bermuda Hundred and the Petersburg campaigns.

ABOVE: Major Martin R. Delany of the 104th United States Colored Troops, which was organized at Beaufort, South Carolina, during the spring of 1865. Major Delany was the first black staff officer in the history of the United States military. General Rufus Saxton ordered Delany to Beaufort to assist him in the organization of two black regiments in South Carolina. The capable Delany earned the rank of lieutenant colonel in March 1865. RIGHT: Officers of the 4th United States Colored Troops pose for the camera at Fort Slocum, part of the extensive network of defenses protecting Washington, D.C., in April 1865.

unbreakable religious faith; they were fervent and moral soldiers who believed that God was on their side. This, in part, explains why African American soldiers performed extremely well in combat, against all odds, and in the most trying circumstances. Colonel Higginson knew as much, and for these qualities he admired the resoluter black men of the 1st South Carolina Volunteers, who had only recently labored as slaves in the Deep South. Higginson described how his African American soldiers were motivated by religious zeal:

"A religious army," "a gospel army," were their frequent phrases. In their prayer-meetings there was always a mingling, often quaint enough, of [the] warlike and the pious…the most reckless and daring fellows in the regiment were perfect fatalists in their confidence that God would watch over them, and that if they died, it would be because their time had come. This almost excessive faith, and the love of freedom and of their families, all cooperated with their pride as soldiers to make them do their duty.

OPPOSITE: The regimental brass band of the 107th United States Colored Troops at Fort Corcoran on Arlington Heights outside Washington, D.C., on November 18, 1865. LEFT: A determined and proud soldier of Colonel Thomas Wentworth Higginson's 1st South Carolina Infantry in this painting by famed artist Don Troiani.

EPILOGUE

The many contributions of African Americans during the Civil War were so crucial and significant that the Union might well have not won the war without them. A quarter of a million escaped slaves and freedmen, or "contrabands," thousands of African American women who assisted the war effort, and more than 200,000 black soldiers in the ranks played a key role in ensuring a decisive Union victory in 1865.

Ironically, however, the role of blacks in the Civil War has been misunderstood and minimized by historians for generations. Only recently has the dramatic story of African Americans and their important contributions from 1861 to 1865 been fully appreciated, adding an inspiring chapter to the annals of Civil War historiography.

However, perhaps the most important contribution of African Americans during the war was that they provided the Union with the moral high ground to turn the war into a struggle for human freedom, while reinvigorating the war effort to ensure victory. This "new birth of freedom" transformed the Civil War from a murderous relentless conflict into the Second American Revolution and a noble crusade, forcing the nation to live up to its promises of liberty and freedom for all Americans.

ABOVE: Soldiers returning from war are reunited with their families and friends at Little Rock, Arkansas, in 1866. RIGHT: Victorious soldiers stand guard over the vanquished in this painting by artist Rick Reeves.

BIBLIOGRAPHY

Adams, Virginia M. *On the Altar of Freedom: A Black Soldier's Civil War Letters from the Front.* New York: Warner Books, 1992.

Aptheker, Herbert. *American Negro Slave Revolts.* New York: International Publishers, 1974.

Burchard, Peter. *One Gallant Rush: Robert Gould Shaw and His Brave Black Regiment.* New York: St. Martin's Press, 1965.

Cornish, Dudley T. *The Sable Arm: Negro Troops in the Union Army: 1861–1865.* New York: Longmans Green & Company, 1956.

Douglass, Frederick. *Narrative of the Life of Frederick Douglass, an American Slave.* Boston: Anti-Slavery Officer, 1845.

Drotning, Phillip T. *Black Heroes in Our Nation's History.* New York: Washington Square Press, 1969.

Duff, John B., and Mitchell, Peter M., ed. *The Nat Turner Rebellion: The Historical Event and the Modern Controversy.* New York: Harper & Row Publishers, 1971.

Duncan, Russell, ed. *Blue-Eyed Child of Fortune: The Civil War Letters of Colonel Robert Gould Shaw.* New York: Avon Books, 1992.

Durden, Robert F. *The Gray and the Black: The Confederate Debate on Emancipation.* Baton Rouge: Louisiana State University Press, 1972.

Edmonds, David C. *The Guns of Port Hudson: The Investment, Siege, and Reduction.* Lafayette: Arcadiana Press, 1984.

Edwards, Frank S. *A Campaign in New Mexico.* Philadelphia: Carey & Hart, 1847.

Elkins, Stanley M. *Slavery, a Problem in American Institutional and Intellectual Life.* Chicago: The University of Chicago Press, 1974.

Emilio, Luis F. *A Brave Black Regiment: The History of the 54th Massachusetts, 1863–1865.* New York: Da Capo Press, 1995.

Fleming, Thomas. *Liberty! The American Revolution.* New York: Viking, 1997.

Genovese, Eugene D. *From Rebellion to Revolution: Afro-American Slave Revolts in the Making of the Modern World.* Baton Rouge: Louisiana State University Press, 1979.

Gladstone, William A. *United States Colored Troops, 1863–1867.* Gettysburg: Thomas Publications, 1990.

Glatthaar, Joseph T. *Forged in Battle: The Civil War Alliance of Black Soldiers and White Officers.* New York: Meridian Books, 1991.

Higginson, Thomas Wentworth. *Army Life in a Black Regiment.* New York: Collier Books, 1962.

Jordan, Winthrop D. *The White Man's Burden: Historical Origins of Racism in the United States.* Oxford, Ohio: Oxford University Press, 1974.

Kaplan, Sidney. *The Black Presence in the Era of the American Revolution 1700–1800.* New York: New York Graphic Society, 1973.

Lofton, John. *Denmark Vesey's Revolt: The Slave Plot That Lit a Fuse to Fort Sumter.* Kent, Ohio: Kent State University Press, 1983.

Longacre, Edward G. *Army of Amateurs: General Benjamin F. Butler and the Army of the James, 1863–1865.* Mechanicsburg, Pa.: Stackpole Books, 1997.

McPherson, James M. *The Negro's Civil War: How American Negroes Felt and Acted During the War for the Union.* New York: Vintage Books, 1965.

Mahon, John K. *History of the Second Seminole War 1835–1842.* Gainesville: University of Florida Press, 1967.

Nell, William C. *Services of Colored Americans in the Wars of 1776 and 1812.* New York: AMS Press, 1976.

Quarles, Benjamin. *The Negro in the American Revolution 1770–1800.* Chapel Hill: University of North Carolina Press, 1972.

Rollins, Richard, ed. *Black Southerners in Gray: Essays on Afro-Americans in Confederate Armies.* Murfreesboro, Tenn.: Southern Heritage Press, 1994.

Rudwick, Bracey Meier. *Free Blacks in America: 1800–1860.* Belmont, Calif.: Wadsworth Publishing Company, 1971.

Wiley, Bell Irvin. *Embattled Confederates: An Illustrated History of Southerners at War.* New York: Harper & Row Publishers, 1964.

Wilson, Joseph T. *The Black Phalanx.* New York: Arno Press, 1968.

Wise, Stephen R. *Gate of Hell: Campaign for Charleston Harbor, 1863.* Columbia: University of South Carolina Press, 1994.

PHOTO CREDITS

Front jacket: Painting by Don Troiani (photo courtesy of Historical Art Prints Ltd., Southbury, CT)

Back jacket photography: Corbis-Bettmann

Archive Photos: p. 113; The Museum of the City of New York: p. 48 bottom

Art Resource: ©National Portrait Gallery, Smithsonian Institution: p. 8, ©Scala: p. 31 (inset)

©Christopher C. Bain: pp. 14 left, 30 left, 52 left, 72 left, 88 left

Brown Brothers: pp. 18, 24 top, 106

Corbis-Bettmann: pp. 13, 16, 17 bottom, 25, 26 both, 29 bottom, 34–35, 38 bottom, 46–47, 49, 78, 80 top, 83, 86–87, 89 (inset), 95 right, 96, 100, 109, 116 left, 116 right–117, 122, front and back endpapers

The Greenwich Workshop, Inc.: *Attack on Battery Wagner* by Tom Lovell ©1993, Courtesy of The Greenwich Workshop, Inc., Shelton, CT 06484: pp. 68–69

Library of Congress: pp. 24 bottom, 28(#B8171-221), 48 top, 50 all, 54, 74, 108 bottom

Massachusetts Commandery Military Order of the Loyal Legion and the U.S. Army, Military History Institute: pp. 29 top, 36, 38 top, 39, 45 both, 94–95 left, 105, 118 left, 118 right–119

Massachusetts Historical Society: pp. 55 both, 56, 57, 59, 61, 62 left, 66, 67, 70–71, 101 top left, 101 bottom

Collection of The Michael Friedman Publishing Group: pp. 4–5, 12, 14 right–15 (background), 27, 30 right–31 (background), 32, 33, 42–43, 52 right–53 (background), 53 (inset), 58, 60, 64, 84, 88 right–89 (background), 91, 97, 102–103, 104, 110, 111, 114–115

The Museum of the Confederacy, Richmond, VA: pp. 81, 85; Courtesy of the Library of Congress: pp. 44, 98 left, 98 right–99, 101 top right , 120; Copied by Katherine Wetzel: pp. 73 (inset), 76, 82; Copied by E.W. Holsinger: p. 79

Naval Historical Foundation, Basic Collections: pp. 92–93 all

North Wind Picture Archive: pp. 17 top, 19 both, 21, 65, 112

Painting by Rick Reeves, photo courtesy of Hans Kaczmarek: pp. 1, 2–3, 37, 123

Picture Collection, The Branch Libraries, The New York Public Library: p. 80 bottom

Photographs and Prints Division, Schomburg Center for Research in Black Culture, The New York Public Library, Astor, Lenox and Tilden Foundations: pp. 10–11, 20 both, 41, 62 right, 63, 72 right–73 (background), 77, 82 right, 90, 107

A. Thorpe: Photo courtesy of *The Civil War Times Illustrated:* p.75

Painting by Don Troiani, photo courtesy of Historic Art Prints: pp. 40, 51, 121

UPI/Corbis-Bettmann: pp. 9, 15 (inset), 22, 23

West Point Museum Collections, U.S. Military Academy: p. 108 top

INDEX